To Bob & Frank
with love
and best wishes.

[signature] 3/17

A
FORTUNATE
LIFE

Fred H. Rohn

ARCHWAY
PUBLISHING

Copyright © 2017 Fred H. Rohn.

All rights reserved. No part of this book may be used or reproduced by any means, graphic, electronic, or mechanical, including photocopying, recording, taping or by any information storage retrieval system without the written permission of the author except in the case of brief quotations embodied in critical articles and reviews.

This book is a work of non-fiction. Unless otherwise noted, the author and the publisher make no explicit guarantees as to the accuracy of the information contained in this book and in some cases, names of people and places have been altered to protect their privacy.

Drumthwacket photo by Virginia Hill; owned by The Foundation

Archway Publishing books may be ordered through booksellers or by contacting:

Archway Publishing
1663 Liberty Drive
Bloomington, IN 47403
www.archwaypublishing.com
1 (888) 242-5904

Because of the dynamic nature of the Internet, any web addresses or links contained in this book may have changed since publication and may no longer be valid. The views expressed in this work are solely those of the author and do not necessarily reflect the views of the publisher, and the publisher hereby disclaims any responsibility for them.

Any people depicted in stock imagery provided by Thinkstock are models, and such images are being used for illustrative purposes only. Certain stock imagery © Thinkstock.

ISBN: 978-1-4808-4165-9 (sc)
ISBN: 978-1-4808-4167-3 (hc)
ISBN: 978-1-4808-4166-6 (e)

Library of Congress Control Number: 2016921025

Print information available on the last page.

Archway Publishing rev. date: 02/07/2017

CONTENTS

Dedication vii
Preface ix

Ancestry 1
Grandparents 8
Parents 24
Growing Up 28
College Life 43
Navy Days 52
Marriage and Family 63
Grandchildren 87
Friends 94
Career Choices 99
Sports 103
Music 114
Community Service 123
Religion 132

Creative Writing and Examples 140

Pride of the Village 142

Vacation 147

Does Your Angel Investor Wear a Halo? 152

Thoughts about the Past 157

Thoughts about the Future 168

DEDICATION

To June, who has been my friend, partner, critic and personal cheerleader for all of my adult years, for her abiding love and understanding. Without her, there would be no story to tell, no book to write.

Fred H. Rohn

Dated 2017

PREFACE

Crafting a personal memoir should, in my view, be more than an ego trip. The nostalgic reminiscences should try to distinguish which events in one's life came to pass purely through circumstance, and those which were influenced by personal decisions.

I have attempted, in this endeavor, to suggest how my one small life fits, as a microcosm, into the fabric of family, friends and an ever changing world environment.

If I am at least partly successful in achieving this goal, perhaps my children, grandchildren, their potential progeny and perhaps a greater audience outside of the family will read this little book and come away with a sense that each of our lives really matters.

ANCESTRY

Including a family tree diagram is often helpful in establishing an understanding of family lineage. For the Rohn family, such a tree would be unusual to the extent of containing odd looking branches. So, here is a description of family relationships, which while it may seem confusing, is the best summary possible.

My Great Grandmother Rohn, in Germany, was married twice. She and her first husband, whose last name was Wvenschenmaier, had three daughters, Katherine, Gretchen and Barbara. After he died, she married a Mr. Rohn, and they had a son in 1816, my grandfather, Fred Rohn Sr.

Now, the lineage gets more confusing. Katherine Wvenschenmaier (Katie) married John Rohn who was a brother to her stepfather. At some point, they emigrated from Germany to the United States and had two children, John Jr. and George. John became a doctor in practice in Newark, New Jersey, and (hold your breath!) married Katherine Harwick, who was the younger sister to my own mother's mother, my Grandmother Hagadorn. So much for charting a family tree!

My Aunt Katie lived in Irvington, New Jersey and we visited with her frequently, often at my grandmother's home. Unlike my grandparents, who spoke without an accent, Aunt Katie spoke with the traces of a German accent. She was always kind and attentive to my brother and me, and gave us each a crisp new two dollar bill at Christmas.

Aunt Katie's other two sisters also emigrated from Germany to the United States. Gretchen married Christian Gloeckler and had a tavern in Plainfield, NJ. They had no children. He always seemed, when I was a boy, to be strict, without humor and stern. Barbara, after her first husband, whose name was Kotterine, died, married Fred Weimer, Sr. Their son, Fred Weimer, Jr. married Ethel. They lived in Madison near to us. They had no children. My brother was an executor of Ethel Weimer's estate, and asked me to help with the administration of it. Fred had died a few years before her death at age ninety-five.

My grandmother's side of the family is less complicated. She was born in Blanfilden Germany in 1873 as Wilhelmina Gehring.

a year, with Marshall Plan money provided by the United States, Lahr was rebuilt, including the four-story Café Bauer, which not only housed the bakery and restaurant, but also was home to the Jürgenmeyer family. When we visited, this family could still not fathom how or why this rebuilding could have happened. They were totally in awe.

Traute's one son, Michael, has been particularly good at communication with our family. He and his wife, Jütta, who have no children, have visited us in Madison, attended my brother's fiftieth wedding anniversary in Florida, and hosted us in Lahr at Michael's sixtieth birthday party. He and Jütta have gone skiing in the Alps with our son Doug, Nancy and their son, Matthew. He remembers every birthday with an email and writes a newsy Christmas letter. Michael is an attorney and an accountant in Lahr.

In many ways, our immediate family's lives have been enriched by knowing our German born relatives.

There is not much background chronicled on my mother's side of the family. Had they kept records, I'm certain there would be lineage dating back to William Penn. I believe both my mother's parents came from Pennsylvania Dutch heritage. Both were from the Allentown, Pennsylvania area. I know my grandmother's maiden name was Harwick, that she had three sisters and a brother. My Grandfather Hagadorn died months before I was born at age sixty-five. He never got to see a grandchild.

My grandfather was twice married. He and his first wife had a son, Verne. After she died at childbirth, my grandfather married my grandmother, Mary Harwick. They had three children, Evelyn (my mother), Russell and Isabel. Verne married Ottilie and they had no children. Isabel married Joe Abrahamson and they had a son, Joseph. Russell and his wife Marian had a son, John. As I write this, none of these relatives is living. My grandmother outlived both of her daughters.

My grandmother's sister, Ida married a man named Shankwailer and lived all her life in Allentown. They had no children. Her brother Jean, who was older, also lived in the Allentown area. I don't remember ever meeting him. My grandmother's sister Katherine, married John Rohn and lived near us in New Jersey. They had two children, Madeline and John. My grandmother's youngest sister, Alice, married a man named Meyer and moved to Detroit. She had a daughter but I don't recall meeting her.

All of these family members were on friendly terms with each other, but didn't spend a lot of time visiting each other. Growing up, and as adults, we saw my Uncle Verne once or twice a year, my Uncle Russell, infrequently, my Aunt Isabel, who lived near us, more often, as well as frequent visits with my Aunt Katherine. My Uncle Verne (more about him later) and my Aunt Katherine (really my great aunt) had more of an impact on my life than the others. I'm separating out my Grandmother Hagadorn for a different group of memories.

GRANDPARENTS

Easter 1945. In back, Mother and Grandmother Hagadorn. Seated, Grandparents Rohn

When I was growing up, my Grandparents Rohn lived in Newark, New Jersey, approximately five miles from our home in Hillside. They had immigrated, separately as teenagers, from different parts of Germany in the early 1890s, arriving in Philadelphia. Each had a relative in the United States to sponsor them, and each had already acquired useful skills, my grandmother as a seamstress, my grandfather, a butcher's apprentice. Both found immediate employment, she as a seamstress for the Wannamaker's store, he as a butcher's aide in the Philadelphia area.

Eventually they met, married, and moved to what is known as the "down neck" section of Newark where they opened a butcher shop. I say "they" opened a shop because my grandmother took an active management role in the operation. My grandfather concentrated on buying, cutting, and selling meat. Times were good and they prospered, moving first to 17th Street, away from the center of Newark and then to the last street on the South Orange border of Newark, to a two-family home at 24 Dover Street. There they lived the remainder of their lives: he until felled by a stroke at age seventy-seven; she at age eighty-eight after falling and breaking her hip three years earlier.

As a boy and man I respected and revered my grandparents. I never disliked visiting them. My grandmother had a closet full of toys which occupied my brother and me when we were young. As I got older, I found that I could actually carry on a conversation with my Grandmother Rohn. She knew, probably from her experience at raising three boys of her own, what boys were interested in and was able to relate to what interested me at the different stages of my growth.

My Grandfather Rohn was quiet, but always pleasant. I don't think I developed as strong a rapport with him as with my grandmother. That's just the way it was.

Grandma Rohn was a good German cook. She loved to host Sunday night suppers when I was young. Pot roast, noodles with gravy, and sometimes with home-made dumplings, was a specialty. I never was served a meal by her that I didn't thoroughly enjoy. Grandpa's job was limited to cutting the meat, helping carry the platters from the kitchen to the dining room and then helping wash and dry the dishes after the meal.

There was a Leslie Thrasher print on the kitchen wall which my grandmother loved. The scene is a butcher shop store counter. The proprietor, with an innocent face was slyly pushing down on a scale between him and the customer on which a chicken was being weighed. The customer, a kindly looking older lady, resembling my grandmother, was intently looking at the scale while her own hand was pushing the scale up, lowering the weight. There is no caption on the print. My grandmother thought the picture was hilarious. She never considered using the picture as a lesson to my brother and me on the sins of cheating, which might have been a temptation to some grandparents.

My grandmother was obviously a good business person. During the Depression of the 1930s, she extended credit to the butcher shop patrons, all of whom she got to know well, sometimes through common membership in the German Lutheran Church in Newark.

I think in many cases she controlled her customers' budgets. She knew where they worked and insisted on payment terms which were realistic and steady. My grandfather kept cutting the meat in his white apron. They were an effective combination. She was the boss and he was just as happy about that.

My father was the eldest of three boys. The middle brother, Herbert, became an attorney and worked his entire working career as did Leslie, the youngest brother, for the Prudential Insurance Company, in Newark. Herbert and his wife, Lillian Alla, owned a home in Newark after they married, located about a mile from my grandparents. They had no children and moved to Boca Raton, Florida in their retirement years. My Uncle Leslie married Doris Sheely and they owned a home in Bloomfield. Both my uncles outlived their wives and died in their mid-eighties.

Uncle Leslie and Doris had two children, Shirley and Charles, a few years younger than my brother and me. Both are living as I write this. I'm in touch with Charles, but not with Shirley. They are my only cousins on my father's side of the family.

As an illustration of my grandmother's spunkiness, I'll relate the following anecdote. At one time my father was the general manager of an ice cream manufacturer and distributor. He remarked one day that his company had recently lost the account of the confectionary store my grandmother frequented near their home. My grandmother decided to act. She nonchalantly walked into the store and ordered a quart of Dolly Madison ice cream. "I'm sorry, Mrs. Rohn, but we aren't selling that brand any more, but we have another kind, Breyers, which is even better." "What?" demanded my grandmother. "You don't have Dolly Madison ice cream? I'm taking all my business elsewhere." And then she stormed out of the store.

She told a couple of her friends about all this, and two of them had the same conversation with the now flustered store owner. She related the entire tale to my father with great glee. I don't know whether he ever got his one-time customer back. But my grandmother had a great time.

A more serious encounter occurred in the midst of the war against Germany. My grandparents had assimilated into United

States culture quickly and had become U.S. citizens as quickly as they could. My grandmother boasted that she voted in every election from the beginning of women's suffrage to her death. Though she continued to belong to a German Lutheran church, she attended their English language services. They spoke only English to their children and then to their grandchildren. Their English was impeccable, without an accent, developed over years of practice.

Both my grandparents had family in Germany. They were in regular contact with these relatives by letter. Additionally my grandmother sent frequent CARE packages to family in Germany, boxes containing clothes and other necessities in short supply in Europe.

One day in early 1943, two strangers rang the doorbell. My grandmother, who was alone, ushered in two young FBI agents who had identified themselves at the door. They wanted to ask her some questions, they said.

My grandmother said she'd be glad to answer any questions they might have, but she wanted one or both of her two sons to be present. She'd call them and it would take about thirty minutes for them to arrive. The agents said they would wait.

Both my father and Uncle Herbert hurried together to 24 Dover Street. The young agents said that the government was interviewing individuals of German heritage who were regularly communicating with people living in Germany.

My father and uncle told the agents that my grandmother had been a citizen since before they were born, that she had voted in every election since women's suffrage, and that her sisters in Germany needed and appreciated the packages of necessities she regularly sent to them. There would be no interview, they said, and told the agents to leave. The young men quietly departed, and my grandmother never heard anything further from the FBI.

My Grandmother Rohn loved to enter contests. In her later years, this pastime became an important hobby to her. The local daily newspaper, the *Newark Evening News*, ran contests to spur subscriptions, on a recurring basis. Each day there would be a question to be answered by mailing in a coupon. The questions progressively became more difficult to answer, requiring greater research. At some point, everyone was eliminated who had not answered every question correctly. The survivors continued to answer "tie breaker" questions which required even more extensive research to answer. These, my grandmother would review with my Uncle Herbert before submission. The questions at the very end of the "tie breaking" round she found too challenging, and she never won a big prize, although the lesser prizes she did win kept her spirits up.

Her enthusiasm about contests was transferred to me, and as a result, I have continued entering contests as a hobby over my lifetime. I've had good fortune in winning contests. Persistence in entering is the only recommendation I would offer to those who might have an interest.

Grandma Rohn, as I noted previously, had been trained as a girl in Germany to be a seamstress. I don't recall her ever making children's clothes of any kind, but she did add flourishes to her own clothes, such things as bright appliqués sewn onto vests, which she often wore. She liked bright colorful clothes, many of brocade. I never saw her in a housedress.

My grandparents rented the first floor of their home. Their tenant for many years was a City of Newark employee whose job included emptying Newark parking meters. Often the rent was paid in nickels. My grandmother recognized the significance of this, but decided, as a practical matter, to ignore the issue.

I've written primarily about my Grandmother Rohn in these pages. I don't mean to diminish the significance of my grandfather. He was always available to lend a hand, and he was a good listener. He didn't say much, but his presence always indicated his supportive nature. My grandmother had flair and drive and a sense of humor and adventure and she is easier to write about. Quiet, steady people don't make for interesting copy but my grandfather set a tone of family, steadiness and strength that was important.

1946. In back, from left: Fred and Bob. Seated, Grandparents Rohn

One of our family's most memorable moments was the celebration of my grandparents' fiftieth anniversary in 1949. My father and uncles arranged a dinner party in the ballroom of a hotel in downtown Newark. Every family member and many friends and neighbors attended. There was music, a head table where the beaming honorees sat flanked by their three sons, their minister and some Newark dignitaries. Mayor Vincent Murphy attended, gave a rousing speech and stayed the entire evening. To my grandparents, the attendance by the mayor of New Jersey's largest city was a high honor. The theme of his remarks was that it was people like my grandparents who made Newark a great city.

Newark may or may not have been great, but it was an interesting city at the time. Its population was made substantially of immigrants from Italy, Ireland and Germany who had settled there in the early twentieth century. The people tended to congregate in separate districts. There was a significant Jewish population, living primarily in the Weequahic section. Various religions flourished, the cultures clashed, but the population by and large got along with one another. The various factions seemed to rotate mayors – Villani, Ellenstein, Murphy.

Commerce was to a large extent controlled by the Prudential Insurance Company, Mutual Benefit Life Insurance Company, two banks and the breweries. (Newark's water was conducive to beer brewing.) There was a mafia presence, apparently headed by Longie Zwillman, who was known as the only Jewish member of the mafia in a leadership role. He had his own table at the Tavern Restaurant in the Weequahic section of Newark. We often, as a family, ate there, and Longie always came over to say hello to us, as he did with every guest. I didn't know who he was, but he seemed like a nice man. My father always seemed a bit embarrassed by his greetings.

When World War II started, the federal government took over some of the Prudential office buildings and established a government agency there – The Office of Dependency Benefits, which did all the paperwork in providing benefits to the families of servicemen. To staff this agency with the clerical help needed, the federal government provided transportation and housing for several thousand black workers from the south of the United States. This created one more set of diverse cultures to be woven into the fabric of Newark's life.

All went relatively well with this effort until the war ended and the government agency was closed down, leaving a lot of displaced southerners without employment. In a postwar growing economy, it was not enough to provide jobs to a steadily growing population.

Her father was Johann Goerg Gehring and her mother was Rosine Margarite Dieterich. They died in Germany in 1909 and 1934 respectively. She had four sisters and two brothers. Sophie and Fritz were her only siblings who emigrated. Sophie married Fred Boelson and lived in Buffalo, New York. They had a daughter, Emma, who never married. Fritz died at age twenty-seven in Philadelphia. He was three years older than my grandmother. I don't know if they emigrated at the same time. I'm inclined to think so. In any event, he died two years before my grandparents married in 1899.

My grandmother's sister Luise, ten years younger, married Carl Bauer in 1916. They established a bakery/konditery in Lahr, Germany, a quaint town along the Rhine River on the edge of the Black Forest. They owned the property in the business section of town. They were both a wholesaler and retailer of home made baked goods. Their restaurant seated fifty people, and it was a gathering place for locals to have coffee, cake, and chat. Eventually, one of their daughters, Traute, together with her husband Helmut Jürgenmeyer, took over the operation and their son Felix continued the business until it was sold.

June and I, together with our four children, visited this family when Rick and Kathy were young teenagers. Traute and Helmut's four children were exactly the same ages as our children. Helmut was away when we visited, so we never met him. But the children got along fine and the German clan was happy to practice their English with their American cousins. Our two older children went to school with the older German cousins. Kathy gave an impromptu talk in English class, which apparently was a big hit.

Interestingly, Traute looked and talked just like my grandmother. One would have thought they could have been twins, although, of course, they were a generation apart.

Traute's younger sister, Ruth, and her husband Wilhelm Eichner, lived nearby. They had no children of their own, but were devoted to Traute's family. They were included in most of the activities during our visit.

Lahr is a charming town. It is not far away from the Swiss border. For the most part it escaped the bombing rounds of World War II, since it had no military or strategic value. By mistake, most think, at the very end of the war it was bombed by the Royal Air Force (RAF) and some of the downtown area was destroyed, including the Café Bauer, as it was named.

Shortly thereafter, the war ended. One American soldier marched into Lahr, announcing the end of the hostilities. Within

To some, the government, which had created opportunity on one hand, failed to provide opportunities to those who lost their jobs when the government agency shut down.

My mother's mother, Grandma Hagadorn, was also an important family member. My grandfather had died in 1925, months before I was born, so he never was a grandfather. He was the railroad station agent for the village of Lockwood, New York, eight miles from Waverly, New York, on the border of Pennsylvania. He served on the ruling council of the village for many years. He was proud to be a notary public, which was as close to being a lawyer as there was in those days in an isolated village such as Lockwood. He and the postmaster, who also was the proprietor of the only grocery store in the village, were the most important people in town. In the 1920s, four local trains stopped in Lockwood each day, two in each direction. They picked up and left off passengers who were going into town. The railroad, The Lehigh Valley, crossed Pennsylvania and New York State and terminated in Buffalo. Lockwood was on the district main line.

Each day, an express train would pick up mail as it sped past the local stations by grabbing, mechanically, a pouch of outgoing mail which the station agent hung by a contraption beside the tracks.

One day in 1925, my grandfather, while hanging up the mail pouch, suffered a massive stroke and died on the spot.

My Grandmother Hagadorn was born and raised in Allentown, Pennsylvania. Mary Harwick was of Pennsylvania Dutch ancestry. She married my grandfather in about 1897. His first wife died a year or so earlier, leaving my grandfather with an infant son, Verne.

So, my grandmother as a newly-wed, acquired a baby as well as a husband. My mother, Evelyn, was born in 1899, followed by my Uncle Russell and Aunt Isabelle over the following five years.

The four children each attended the one room schoolhouse in Lockwood, which was almost directly across the street from their home. There was no high school, so teenagers went by train each day to Waverly for their high school educations.

For my mother's high school years, though, my grandmother chose to send my mother to stay with my grandmother's younger sister, Katherine, who had married John Rohn, a medical doctor, and lived on Clinton Avenue in a big home in Newark. After graduating from Barringer High School in 1917, my mother studied to become a school teacher at the Newark Normal School. It was at a Rohn family gathering that my mother met my father in 1921 or

1922. He was completing a degree in business at night from New York University, while holding a full-time job.

Barringer High School, Newark N.J.

Grandma Hagadorn lived in Lockwood, New York until her four children were married and had established their own families and homes. Eventually she sold her home and rotated staying with her four children until she was eighty-five years old, after which she stayed full time with her son Verne. Both my mother and my Aunt Isabel were ailing with life-ending diseases and Uncle Verne and Aunt Ottilie, with no children were glad to take care of her. My grandmother, sadly, outlived both her daughters.

Since my Grandmother Hagadorn lived with us for several months each year, I got to know her well. She was a very good cook and seamstress, and spent much of her time at our home cooking meals, mending clothes, and embroidering doilies. Our house had more doilies on display than any other home I've ever visited. In addition to her sewing and cooking talents, she had some artistic ability in water color and oil paintings. I don't remember her doing any painting in her later years, but the few paintings I have retained are quite professional. One hangs in our Madison bedroom to this day.

None of my Grandparents Rohn ever owned an automobile and I don't believe either of my grandparents had a driver's license. Apparently, my Grandmother Hagadorn did have a car in her earlier years. She told the story of never having learned to shift the car into reverse gear. Fortunately her home in Lockwood had a circular driveway, and she made certain that when she drove around the village, she parked so that she would never have to back up. I never saw her drive and I doubt if she kept her license in her later years.

Financially, all my grandparents were self-sufficient throughout their lives. Each one owned a home. My Grandmother Hagadorn had a pension from the railroad, and a free lifetime railroad pass which she used on occasion.

My Grandmother Hagadorn had inherited many Pennsylvania Dutch recipes. One of my favorites was dried corn. She would hang ears of corn in the basement. In mid winters she would cut off the dried kernels and boil them with seasoning until they were soft. As a boy, I found this vegetable dish very tasty.

My grandmothers were almost exactly the same age. They saw each other often and got along fine, but never became intimate friends, though they had much in common. I've often wondered about this.

Both my grandmothers were my friends, particularly in my young adult years. They were fun and interesting to be with, never criticized me, nor forced their ideas upon me and my immediate family. My grandfather was quiet. He often seemed to be a spectator rather than a participant, and although he was obviously a steady, family oriented, hard-working father and grandfather, it was my grandmothers who had more influence in my life.

PARENTS

My mother and father met at a family gathering in 1921 or 1922. My mother, Evelyn Hagadorn, was living with her mother's sister, Katherine, in Newark, New Jersey. Aunt Katherine had been married to John Rohn, the son of my Grandfather Rohn's half-sister, so the two families had occasion to meet. John Rohn, a medical doctor, built a substantial practice in Newark, but unfortunately died at age thirty-nine from a ruptured appendix, leaving my Aunt Katherine financially secure, with two small children, my second cousin Madeline and John Jr. (known as Buddy).

My mother had graduated from Barringer High School in Newark and was attending the Newark Normal School, aspiring to be a school teacher.

My father had graduated from East Side High School in Newark, was employed by the Aristocrat Ice Cream Company, and was attending New York University at night, planning on becoming an accountant.

The Pre-Depression 1920s was a period of growth. My parents, when they married in 1924, were able to buy a new home in Hillside, New Jersey, where there was a series of farms lying between Newark and Elizabeth.

My parents had much in common and were well suited to each other. I don't recall them ever having a verbal fight. My mother was stricter, a teetotaler, and got my father to give up smoking cigars. She was serious, but not threatening in her demeanor, and was a great proponent of education, music and the arts. She was also deeply religious, and was actively engaged at the Hillside Presbyterian Church, two blocks away from our home at 46 Hurden Street.

When she married, my mother, who by then had completed her teacher studies, gave up having a career in teaching and, except for some sporadic substitute teaching assignments, never practiced her chosen profession.

My father had started out toward becoming a Certified Public Accountant (CPA); however, he was afforded various other jobs within the Aristocrat Ice Cream Company and at a young age, was promoted to general manager of the Newark facility.

His employer was a subsidiary of the Philadelphia Dairy Products Company and was housed in a former brewery facility in the downtown area of Newark. He obviously had a good business sense and was personally outgoing with intuitive leadership skills.

My mother, on the other hand, was introspective and somewhat shy. They were a good combination with off-setting strengths.

Typically, my father loved sports, particularly baseball, while my mother saw no merit whatsoever in organized sports. I don't remember her ever throwing a ball, playing tennis, or even going for a walk.

My parents' lives were substantially defined by my mother's breast cancer, detected when she was thirty-nine years old, and which eventually spread, killing her at age forty-seven. I was twenty at the time and my brother Bob was eighteen. Our lives were ahead of us.

My father, who had increasingly cared for my mother during her final years of suffering, was distraught, even though he knew her death was coming. He had carefully told me of the dire situation more than a year before her death, so when she did die, it was not so much of a shock, but a sense of sadness.

During her final year, my father employed a practical nurse, Margaret Mitchell, to tend to my mother's needs. Margaret had become a widow at an early age. She had two children, Barbara Jean and Dick who were the same ages as my brother and me. She and my father had much in common and they married in 1948, within weeks of my own wedding to June.

It isn't easy for second wives – step mothers – to fit into existing families, or for those families to embrace a new set of relatives.

But my father's and Peg Mitchell's evoked sympathy in both families, with no evident bitterness or distrust.

Barbara Jean died of a stroke at a reasonably young age, outlived by her mother who went on to become ninety-five years old. She and my father had a very good life together. They were married more years than my father and mother, so I like to think that I was blessed by having two mothers. Significantly, my immediate family has always considered Dick Mitchell as my brother, and we continue to be close to each other's families.

There are further insights to impart about my parents which I'll share in the chapter about my growing up. They were great believers in family values and shared my brother Bob's life and mine with their inspirations.

GROWING UP

Mother and Dad. In front, from left: Bob and Fred

Probably the most memorable event of my earliest years took place when I was halfway through first grade in school. My mother was summoned to meet with the principal of Saybrook School, a two block walk from our home.

The principal's message was clear. There were too many first graders and not enough second graders due to some recent enrollments. Five first graders were being promoted to the second half of second grade, and I was one of them. The principal assured my mother that a great deal of thought had gone into this decision, that I was precocious enough to fit into second grade seamlessly and that a bit more of a challenge would be good for me. My mother objected, but eventually reluctantly accepted this change.

I now was a year younger than most of the others in my class. The principal was right. The adjustment academically and socially was indeed seamless. I never felt younger except in sports, where that one year difference was a very large detriment in being able to excel. There was an advantage, however. When I graduated from high school I had an entire year to attend college before having to go into the Army or Navy, an advantage of substantial importance discussed elsewhere in this book.

Neighbors and neighborhoods contributed to our years of growing up. Hurden Street, where I grew up, was one block long, with approximately sixty three-bedroom, one bath, one-family houses, all newly built, and set on fifty-foot lots with a reasonably wide paved street and sidewalks on both sides.

There were quite a number of children on the street and we congregated each day in good weather on the street to play softball, touch football or roller skate hockey. The street in front of our homes was the only place to play games. Somehow the town had not provided zoning for parks or available fields, and the athletic facilities adjacent to the schools were fenced in and gated during non-school activity hours. So we played in the street.

Most neighbors maintained lawns in the front of their homes. But Mr. and Mrs. Dilks, next to our house on Number 46, had planted elaborate flower gardens in front of their home, including beds of portulaca on the strip between the sidewalk and the curb. Their daughter and son-in-law, Mr. and Mrs. Weeks, lived in the house adjacent to them, and also had extensive front-yard flower gardens. These two related families, one set in their eighties and the other in their fifties, with no children, devoted much of their time to lovingly tending to their gardens.

Invariably, an errant softball or football would find its way into one of these gardens, requiring one of us players to retrieve the ball from amidst the gardens. Sometimes the ball would be hidden within the greenery and we'd have to search through the plantings, often creating irreparable damage to the well-planned and maintained gardens.

Almost daily, while we were playing, a police car would drive up and stop in the middle of our game and the lone driver would call us over to the window of the squad car.

"Got another complaint about you boys tramping on the flowers on private property," he'd invariably say.

"We're just playing in the street. What do you want us to do?" one of us would ask.

"Just move up the street and play there for a while," he'd say.

"But our mothers want us to play in front of our own homes, so they can keep an eye on us," we'd remonstrate.

"Just do me a favor and move up a few homes" would be his response. And he'd quickly drive away. I'm sure he loved this daily call.

I got along very well with Mrs. Dilks. She taught me a lot about gardening, how to sow seeds, water and cultivate flowers and vegetables. As she got older and the upkeep of her gardens threatened to overwhelm her, she hired me to do some of the heavier work in her garden, often paying me in seeds and plants. Eventually I planted a garden of my own in our backyard and applied my entrepreneurial spirit by selling lettuce, beans, corn and tomatoes to our neighbors from a pull wagon, with the phrase "Lettuce Serve You" on an attached cardboard sign.

My ball playing friends noticed that the frequency of complaints to the police lessened when I was playing in the street. My mother called me in on each school day at five p.m. to practice piano, and Mrs. Dilks usually would wait for me to go in the house before calling the police.

On weekends, Mr. Weeks patrolled the two properties and confiscated any errant balls which landed in the gardens. Often, this act stopped the game at hand if there were no other balls available. Mrs. Dilks always returned any balls her family had retrieved directly to me a day or two later.

These clashes continued throughout my grammar and high school years and culminated in the fall of 1942, at a time of great patriotic fervor as World War II escalated.

One Saturday afternoon, a few of us were tossing a football around in the street and were joined by a young man, only a few years older than we were, who lived several houses up the street. He had recently joined the Navy, was assigned to a destroyer on patrol duty in the Atlantic Ocean, and had a weekend pass while his ship was being refueled at the Brooklyn Navy Yard. Not long after he joined us, a police patrol car pulled up. The officer was not much older than our Navy buddy, and he told us we were making too much noise. The Navy man whipped out his Navy ID tag, and yelled at the dumbstruck policeman, "Here I am on forty-eight hours leave while protecting our country, and you're telling me to be quieter while playing football on my own street. You should be ashamed of yourself."

The officer rolled up his window after muttering something about "taking it easy" and pulled away. I don't know what he reported to his superiors at the police station and what conversation took place with the complaining neighbors, but I don't recall any more police visits while we were playing in the street.

In today's world, a TV investigative reporter would have fun with this event on the local six o'clock news.

There's a more serious note to this little story. These confrontations could have been avoided if the house developers had been required to put aside land for parks and athletic fields as part of their building operations. An entire town was built without any recreational space other than fenced-in school yards. Master planning has made great strides in the past hundred years in this area.

This is a good time to say a few words about my brother Bob, two years and four days my junior. He had different interests than I did. He didn't like team sports and seldom participated in our street games. We both had bicycles, which were in constant use.

I thought of bicycling as transportation. Bob thought of it as a sport and he lovingly cared for his bike and went on little riding adventures with his friends. Bob loved horseback riding. I hated it. When we attended summer camp, I always gave him my once-a-week horseback riding class. Later in life, Bob developed a love for antique cars and worked on their motors. I avoided looking under the hood of a car if I could help it.

I don't think it is easy being a younger brother. My parents recognized this and sent Bob to a private day school, The Pingry School, to separate us. This was a good idea and it served to create self-confidence in Bob. Bob worked as a salesman for a cardboard manufacturer his entire business life and when he retired, was the most senior employee in the company. His "gift of gab" and ability to relate to people was a strength in his sales career. One of Bob's finest achievements was his care for our stepmother when she was in her nineties and living near him and Joan in Fort Myers, Florida. Bob and Joan had no children of their own, and he took a great interest in our children and grandchildren. We had different interests and strengths, but were always steadfast in our devotion to each other.

I don't recall studying much at school or doing a lot of homework. I'm sure my mother oversaw my homework. She was very organized herself and taught me to be organized and how to study. After school, each day during the week, my brother and I could play outside until five p.m. I'd be in the street with my neighbor chums, and my brother would be off on his bicycle on some adventure.

At five p.m., my mother would call us into the house to practice piano (me) and violin (Bob). Bob invariably got home in time for this music session. If I was at bat in a softball game when my mother called, I had to drop the bat and go into the house. I'm certain my buddies considered my mother as a bit of a tyrant, but I never complained.

Practice was from five to six p.m. each night, dinner was from six to seven p.m., and homework was to be completed before bedtime. Our Dad was on a schedule too. Invariably he arrived home by six p.m. and we all ate dinner together.

My mother was a good cook and our meals were always tasty. When my Grandmother Hagadorn was staying with us, she added variety to our meals that went beyond mother's desire and perhaps ability to prepare. We always had ice cream for dessert which my Dad brought home from his workplace, packed in dry ice in the days before refrigerators.

As I grew up, I developed a keen interest in creative writing and in entering contests. Sometimes the two interests could be combined and occasionally I was able to satisfy both interests in one activity.

In 1937, the local daily newspaper ran a contest to pick the International League All Star Baseball Team. The Newark Bears played in this league, the highest level of professional baseball beneath the Major Leagues.

The 1937 Bears "Wonder Team" includes, from left to right, the following: (front row) Jimmie Mack (trainer), George McQuinn, Jimmie Gleeson, Francis Kelleher, Joe Beggs, Oscar Vitt (manager), Willard Hershberger, Vito Tamulis, Joe Gordon, Buddy Rosar, and Joe Fixter

1937 Newark Bears "Wonder Team"

That was the first year that the Newark Bears, owned by Jake Rupert, the Newark Brewer, who also owned the New York Yankees, had put together a roster of players which was said by most sports writers to be better than any Major League team except for the Yankees. Atley Donald, Steve Sundra and Vito Tamulis anchored the pitching staff. Charlie Keller, Jimmy Gleeson, and Bob Seeds patrolled the outfield, Frankie Kelleher played multiple infield positions and Buddy Rosar and Will Hershberger were the stalwart catchers. All became Major League players within two years.

The contest seemed easy enough. Pick the best fifteen players (including five pitchers and two catchers), then playing on the various International League Teams, and if your listing was the same as the one being chosen by the newspaper's sports reporters, you would win a cash prize and a trip to the hometowns of each of the League's teams. There were about 200 players eligible. I had watched a number of games and had all the up-to-date statistics to rely upon. I was able to eliminate 150 players from the potential all-star pool and I was pretty sure of six players who were standouts. I did my own ratings of each player and put together twenty-five possible combinations, all of which I submitted as entries into the contest, feeling pretty good about my selections. When the results were revealed, a couple of my entries had thirteen of the fifteen names, not good enough even for honorable mention. I had all of the fifteen players' names in my two ratings, but didn't have the right combinations. I was disappointed but realized it might have taken more than 200 entries to achieve the winning combination.

As a high school sophomore, my history teacher, Frank Hill, included another newspaper contest as a homework assignment. The contest, sponsored by Newark's weekend paper, *The Sunday Call*, consisted of an essay entitled "What the Reconstruction of Williamsburg, Virginia Means to Me". At the time, the Rockefeller family had just completed rebuilding a portion of Williamsburg into what it had been like in the pre-Revolutionary times. The prizes, one allotted to a high school boy and one to a high school girl, was a cruise from New York to Norfolk, Virginia and several days of all-expenses-paid sightseeing in the new tourist destination in Williamsburg. Each prize winner would be accompanied by a parent.

Everyone in Mr. Hill's History class was required to submit an essay to him, following the contest outline. He would then grade them and submit the four essays he considered best into the newspaper's contest.

I worked hard on my essay, encouraged by both my parents. My mother insisted I research the subject at the local library, but otherwise neither Dad nor Mother critiqued my essay.

I didn't make the top four in Mr. Hill's mind. I thought my submission was good, so I asked my school teacher-trained mother to read it. She thought it was good too and encouraged me to submit it into the contest anyway, which I did. When the announcement in the newspaper named me as the contest winner, a slightly embarrassed Mr. Hill congratulated me warmly. The trip was wonderful and I enjoyed the praise which my family and friends offered.

Years later, when I was just expanding my accounting career, I entered another writing contest. This was a larger endeavor, a full-length book on any aspect of accounting. The sponsor was the leading publisher of business publications at the time, the Prentice Hall Corporation, and was open to anyone in the world. The prize included a substantial cash amount and royalties on book sales. I wrote a book addressed to accountants entitled, *How To Make Your Services Worth More*.

I won the contest and the book was a critical and financial success. One humorous side note of this achievement deserves telling. The accounting firm where I was employed had a policy that staff members could not keep any accounting fees they might earn by doing work on the side, but would have to turn such fees into the firm. I, as did all employees, had signed such an agreement.

When I asked the senior partner in the firm about how proceeds from the book were affected by the directive I had signed, he thought for a moment and said, "No, they're your profits. Book sales don't fit the definition of outside work that competes with our usual services." I could tell he was annoyed, though, that one of his reasonably new staff members had just managed to collect a fee more than five times that person's annual salary.

I went on to write two other books on the accounting subject, neither of which achieved the financial results of the first book.

The vignettes in this chapter illustrate the basically normal, family-oriented activities of a typical boy during the Depression years of the 1930s. We were more fortunate than some. My father had a good, steady job. The family could afford summer camp, music classes, and dinner in a restaurant on Sunday.

In high school, I was the pianist in the school orchestra, had the male lead in the senior play, headed the National Honor Society and was an editor of our class yearbook. I also had a full time girlfriend, June Chadwick, who lived two city blocks away. When we were seniors we went somewhere each Friday and Saturday night. One of our best recurring dates was roller skate dancing at a local indoor rink, an activity that no longer exists. We had lots of friends and were very happy during these years. June and I seldom had an argument. She did complain, however, when I rode her home on my bicycle, that her "seat" on the bicycle bar was uncomfortable. But I don't ever remember her turning down a ride with me.

For some reason, as a teenager, I got along with girls. I guess I was a good listener because several confided in me about their worries, mostly boys. Since I had a girlfriend, I guess it was easier for them to talk to me. I have one poignant example. At the very end of my sophomore year, at a school dance, before I started dating June, a girl I knew and I were dancing and she said to me, "I've got something to tell you. I'm not coming back to school next year. I have to get a job. My mother says we have to have more money."

"You can't do that. It's not right. You're ruining your future," I responded.

"I know," she blurted out and burst into tears. I didn't know what to do or say. One of the teacher chaperones observed her crying uncontrollably, and confronted me.

"What did you say to this girl to make her cry? You'll have to leave."

"No, no," the girl objected. "He didn't do anything. I'll be all right."

Gradually she regained her composure. We said little the rest of the evening and I walked her to her house in complete silence.

"Thanks," she said, kissed my cheek and went into the house. I never saw her again.

By the time I graduated from high school, June and I were spending a lot of time together. We would be immediately separating as I went off to college. She was going to business college and would be living at home. Would our relationship survive the taking of separate paths? We never discussed it, but deep down inside me the question was troublesome.

Fred H. Rohn. Hillside High School graduation, 1943

COLLEGE LIFE

My civilian college life commenced on July 1, 1943, just a few days after high school commencement activities. Men's colleges throughout the country were facing heavily depleted enrollments. Most able bodied young men were in government service. The war draft started at age eighteen and the only college civilian students were those in pre-medical, pre-ministerial studies or were under eighteen, as I was, or were physical unable to enter the draft. So, all ninety of those starting college at Colgate that hot summer day, fell into one of these four categories.

Colgate University, Hamilton, N.Y.

I had chosen Colgate University to attend for the unimportant reason that it was farther away from home than Princeton and not as far as Dartmouth, the other schools to which I had applied for admission and was accepted. I should note that it was easy for a relatively bright young man to get into college in 1943. All the colleges needed students and were relying upon various officer training programs sponsored by the Army, Navy, Marines and Air Corps, to maintain solvency.

The supply of professors and teachers was also depleted. Colgate had recalled retired professors to teach again. They gave up their retirement years to aid the war effort in this way.

I arrived at Colgate with one suitcase. Most of my gear had been shipped in a big steamer trunk. Actually, my train from Newark, New Jersey dropped me off at Earlville, New York, eight miles from Hamilton, the village in which Colgate was located. The Dean of Students himself, Carl Kallgren, picked me up at the Earlville station and drove me to the campus. I wonder how many freshmen at college today are picked up in person by their school's top administrator!

Hamilton is set in a valley which captures heat in the summer, and snow and cold temperatures in the winter. There was no air conditioning in any of the dormitories or classrooms so we freshmen sweated a lot that summer of 1943. This was a time before shorts became popular, so that daily dress was a collared shirt and long pants. The summer of 1943 was the first summer school semester Colgate had ever held and the heat was overbearing.

All the civilian students lived in dormitories inasmuch as the fraternity houses had been leased for use by the various federal officer training programs. It was a bit odd that students who had joined fraternities were living in dormitories while Navy and Marine officer candidates, most of whom were not fraternity members, lived in the fraternity houses which, in general, were more spacious. I did join a fraternity, Delta Upsilon (DU), but despite being on campus for two years, I never lived in the DU fraternity house.

Colgate University campus

There were no scheduled social activities during this period of time. Transportation restrictions eliminated the possibility of arranging for dates with girls and there were no concerts or speakers scheduled.

Our entertainment primarily consisted of attending the local movie, which regularly offered Hopalong Cassidy westerns. The plots were similar movie to movie. We had our fill of these.

An important source of entertainment were the school sports teams, primarily football and baseball. The teams weren't very good. Recruiting didn't exist. My first college football game as a spectator was Colgate versus Army at West Point that fall. Somehow busloads of students found their way to the game despite travel restrictions. The Army team did have obvious recruiting, and we watched as the backfield tandem of Blanchard and Davis ran ramshackle over hapless Colgate 42-0.

The National Collegiate Athletic Association had ruled that Navy and Marine officer candidates could play on the varsity teams at the schools to which they had been assigned. The only restriction was that a professional athlete could not participate in the sport of his profession.

As it turned out, Otto Graham, the star quarterback for the Cleveland Browns of the National Football League (NFL), was assigned to an officer training unit at Colgate. He was not permitted to play football for Colgate, but he did join the basketball team that winter. I was just a scrub player and manager for the team that winter. Otto Graham was a good athlete and could shoot a basketball with precision, but years of playing the more rough and tumble game of football had ill-prepared him for the finesse which basketball required. As a result, he continually committed fouls which greatly diminished his basketball prowess. I remember that he was highly frustrated over this.

The only other celebrity I recall being at Colgate at the time was Bob Eberly, the vocalist for the Jimmy Dorsey dance orchestra. Best known for his hit records with Helen O'Connell, he sang for the orchestra at June's and my senior prom party which was held at the opening of the Terrace Room in Newark. I always wanted to ask him if he remembered that night. Many celebrities attended, and it was the night when Jimmy Dorsey introduced a young, nervous female singer, Kitty Kallen. I always wanted to ask Bob Eberly if he remembered that special night. But I never had the opportunity.

I don't remember any particular feeling of freedom being away from home for the first protracted period of time. I had spent several summers at camp in the Pocono Mountains, so I had some experience away from the watchful eyes of parents. My parents had gradually given me considerable responsibility and freedom to make my own decisions. I came to appreciate this enlightened approach and have attempted to follow their example with my own family.

It was during this period that I took up the card game of bridge. It was intellectually stimulating and captured a certain amount of comradeship and competitiveness. I don't play much anymore, but appreciate all aspects of the game and am sorry that the next generations have not taken to it as much as we did. To me, it's a much more satisfying activity than video games.

When I arrived at Colgate, the school had recently installed a new president, Everett Case. Although I couldn't properly judge it at the time, I later concluded that he was ideal for the job. An academic nature at heart led him to an overhaul of the curriculum, and he installed what became known as the Case Core Curriculum, which added meaningful modernization to the learning process.

Dr. Case was well respected by the faculty (no small feat at most colleges), alumni and the student body. And he went on to serve Colgate as President for many years. As Colgate students, we didn't interface with him much, but his presence on the campus was visible and he extended a thoughtful, kindly approach to those of us who met with him. Dr. Case was an excellent administrator as well, and his political connections with the federal government helped Colgate's college strategy during the war years. Many years later, at my fiftieth college reunion, I suggested, as chair of the reunion committee, that the traditional class gift be in the form of a scholarship entitled "The Everett Case Scholarship". At the time, President Case, long-retired and well into his nineties, was still living in a home outside of Utica, New York.

Case was unable physically to attend the dedication of this scholarship in person at Colgate, and so a contingency of us traveled to present him with the honor at his home. He greeted us warmly, apologized that he was unable to travel to Colgate for the ceremony, and accepted the award graciously. We had a cup of tea with him. He didn't say a lot more except to indicate that the date of our visit coincided with his seventy-fifth graduation date from Princeton and that he believed he was the only one living from his class. I'll always remember him as a role model. He had a wonderful marriage to his wife Josephine, who spent all those years with him at Colgate. She, herself was a scholar who quietly did some teaching at Colgate.

By February 1944, I had completed my freshman year without having any time off. Approaching my eighteenth birthday, I knew I had to make a decision about entering military service. So, just before I turned eighteen, I enlisted in the Naval Reserve. I preferred the Navy over the Army for some vague reasons. Now, my parents were in favor of the decision. I could not enter the V-12 Navy College Training Program any longer, having given up that opportunity a year earlier. So I left Colgate in February of 1944, and by the end of April, I was at boot camp at Sampson, New York. As luck would have it, I was back at Colgate in the V-12 program as recounted elsewhere in this book, and only missed one semester's time.

As I think about it now, my one year of civilian life at Colgate was one of growing up. I found I could do college work and had learned how to study. The year separated June and me and tested our relationship. We wrote to each other weekly (there were no cell phones, email or texting to provide more frequent communication opportunities). The war created an environment in which partying and frivolity was non-existent. I don't know how to compare this with college life today. While the differences are substantial, I'm not certain my experiences lacked opportunities which really mattered in the long run.

NAVY DAYS

Although I served in the Navy for more than two years during World War II, I can't really suggest that I had much to do with the war, nor, for that matter, life in the service as it is broadly defined.

Except for two weeks in boot camp at Sampson, New York, I spent my entire Navy career in college, studying what I had started to major in as a civilian – English. World War II ended simultaneously with my being commissioned an ensign and being released from active duty. How all this fortuitous experience came about may be of some interest.

I had just celebrated my seventeenth birthday when I graduated from Hillside High School, one year younger than I would have been had I not skipped a grade early in my schooling.

In 1942, the U.S. Navy launched a vast officer training program. Premised on the concept that winning World War II in the Pacific would require thousands of small landing crafts island hopping their way to Japan, some of us, as high school seniors, took the test for entry into this program (the V-12 Program) and some few of us were told we had the scores necessary to enter the program, which included at least six semesters of college.

My mother quite naturally refused to let me join the Navy this way, suggesting that the war might be over by the time I was eighteen, which was the age all able bodied males were drafted into the military.

So I went from high school directly to Colgate University and completed my freshman year before I was eighteen.

The war wasn't over in April 1944, so I enlisted in the Navy rather than await being drafted into the Army. At that time, the V-12 Program had no civilian openings anymore.

My mother, of course, was unhappy about my going into the armed services, but there really was no choice unless I planned to be either a doctor or clergyman, professions in which I had no interest.

So, late one evening, I boarded a troop train at Grand Central Station and headed for Sampson, New York. Those on the train were a combination of eighteen-year-olds like me and mid-thirty-five-year-olds, who had opted to go into the Navy instead of the Army.

Many of the young reservists were jubilant about the adventure that they had embarked upon and celebrated throughout the long ride with much drinking and noise making. I didn't feel so elated, so I fell asleep despite all the activity that was taking place.

We arrived at Sampson at daybreak. We were each given an apple and told we'd get some food later on, but that first we'd have to take IQ tests. Few of the eighteen-year-olds were alert enough for this exercise. The mid thirty-five-year-olds hadn't taken any tests for many years and had forgotten how. I was the only one of the group who had been to college, and I had just completed my freshman year finals. So I had an advantage.

Sampson was a busy, sprawling Navy facility with shortages of uniforms, food and activities for us. We did a lot of drilling and learned that it was a good idea not to volunteer for anything.

About the third day there, our corporal called us to order and asked if anyone knew the Dewey Decimal System. I had learned this library filing procedure while at Colgate, so I raised my hand, ignoring the advice on volunteering. As a result, I was assigned to the base library where I spent most of the rest of my two weeks in boot camp.

Except for one other member of our unit, all the other recruits were assigned Kitchen Patrol (KP) or latrine duty, not exactly fun jobs. The other recruit was Jack Philips, a baseball player who, at the time he was called into service, was the third baseman for the Newark Bears, the farm team for the New York Yankees. Philips was being groomed to be the successor to Red Rolfe on the Yankees. He was assigned to the Sampson baseball team.

Sampson had a great baseball team that year. They played various Major League teams on off-days and usually beat them. It was the general consensus that the Sampson team could have won the pennant that year if they had been in the Major Leagues. Johnny Vander Meer (of double no-hitter fame) and Ernie White were their two star pitchers. I got to know Jack Philips a bit because we were assigned bunks alphabetically and his bed was adjacent to mine. We both quietly laughed about being the only two members not on KP or latrine duty.

Like many other athletes, the war dampened their ability to further their career. Jack never became a regular for the Yankees. His best years as an athlete were spent in service.

My Uncle Verne worked for the Delaware and Lackawanna Railroad and was the station agent at Sampson during the war years. This was a highly coveted job because the union contract that the station agents had with the railroad included the agent getting a commission on all freight flowing through the station, and Sampson got a lot of freight. I think my uncle made as much in those years as the president of the railroad.

My Uncle Verne also got to know all the top officers at Sampson in connection with his agent's role. These relationships played a part on one adventure in which I was the central participant.

On the first Sunday I was at Sampson, at morning roll call, the corporal in charge, reading from his orders, informed me that I was to report immediately to the commander's office. "What had I done?" I wondered.

In the commander's office building, I faced a non-smiling lieutenant. "You have an uncle named Verne Hagadorn?" he asked. "Yessir," I replied.

"All right, get into your dress uniform and go to the gate. Your uncle will be there to take you to lunch."

"But I haven't been issued a dress uniform yet, and I'm also on quarantine because of all the shots I've been given."

The officer thought about this for a minute.

"Here's what you should do," he said. "Lie down in the back seat of that car out there," pointing out the window. "Don't say anything to anybody and I'll drive you out through the gate."

I did as I was told and had a nice lunch with my aunt and uncle. Upon returning to the base in mid-afternoon, I was smuggled back in time to make dinner roll call. The corporal in charge called out my name though, and asked why I had missed noon time roll call. I answered truthfully. He clearly didn't believe me, said he would check out my story and that if I wasn't telling the truth I'd be in trouble. He must have checked, because thereafter he treated me with considerate deference, affirming in awe of my ability to pull off such a stunt.

By far, the most important event of my Navy career took place the next day. Again, I was summoned to the commander's office, this time to be confronted by a young officer whom I had not seen before.

"Rohn" he said. "I hear you've had a year at Colgate. And you did pretty well on your tests. We have an opening in the V-12 Program. Do you know what that is and do you want the assignment?"

"Yes, Sir, I'm familiar with the V-12 Program and certainly would like the assignment."

"Good, there are a number of colleges with V-12 Program. Do you have any preferences?"

"Yes, Sir. I'd be happy to go back to Colgate."

The young officer broke into a smile. "Good choice, Rohn. I graduated from Colgate last year."

I called my parents that night and told them of my good luck. My mother, who was not well, was highly relieved. My father couldn't believe he'd not have to pay Colgate tuition ever again.

And so, uniformed and earning fifty dollars per month, I returned as an apprentice seaman to Colgate University where I moved into a fraternity house and continued my studies, majoring in English for six more semesters, and accumulating more than enough credits to earn a Bachelor of Arts degree.

U.S. Navy Ensign Fred H. Rohn

Colgate had done a great job in integrating civilian campus life with naval programs. The civilian student body primarily consisted of pre-med, pre-ministerial and 4-F (physically impaired) students, overshadowed in numbers by the U.S. program and a few other Navy programs. The Navy commander at Colgate was Omar Held, Dean at the University of Pittsburgh, with a clearly academic leaning. As a commander, he took his Navy role seriously, but followed college precepts and wove them, with President Case's aid, into a combined Navy/collegiate atmosphere which met the needs of all.

Toward the end of my Colgate-Navy tenure, I became editor of the *Colgate Maroon*, the weekly campus newspaper. I thought I'd be sent from Colgate prior to my taking over the editor's role.

One day I was called into see Commander Held. He told me the Navy was keeping me at Colgate for another semester, even though I had enough credits for my degree, so that I could edit the newspaper. I was dumfounded and overjoyed.

My parents also were happy. My father's partly facetious reaction was, "With this kind of thinking, I don't know how we'll win the war."

What I didn't know, and what Commander Held didn't tell me, was that I was too young to be commissioned an officer.

I stayed at Colgate three more months and then completed my officer's training at the Reserve Officers' Training Corps (ROTC) program at the College of the Holy Cross in Worcester, Massachusetts.

Colgate granted me my degree even though there was a rule that the student had to be physically on campus the semester before graduating. I received my degree, was commissioned an ensign, and was released to inactive duty all within a ten-day period. With the war ending, Navy funding was greatly cut by Congress and the Navy no longer needed any twenty-one-year-old ensigns to command landing craft in the Pacific. I remained in the Naval Reserve for several years, was promoted once, and finally was discharged. That was the extent of my government service.

There is one humorous postscript. According to the law, the time spent in the V-12 Program did not count for time in service, according to the draft board, which now decided I should be drafted into the Army. Although the war was over, the draft continued for some time thereafter. By now, I was married and had started my career path and had no desire to go back into service. I pointed out to the volunteers who manned the local draft board that I was a naval officer on inactive duty and couldn't very well be drafted into the Army. "That's what the law says," stipulated the draft board. "Maybe you'll have to go back into the Navy to get your time in." I pointed out that the Navy had released me to inactive duty because they didn't need me and didn't have the funds to pay me. The board continued to maintain that I had to go back into service under the law, and I stated that this wasn't possible or practical under the circumstances.

I tried to enlist their sympathy. "This whole situation is upsetting my wife. Her baby is due in a few weeks and I'm worried about her."

"Your wife's pregnant," one draft board member practically yelled. "Why didn't you say so? We aren't drafting fathers. Get us a doctor's note saying your wife is expecting and the matter is ended." The letter was forthcoming and the question was put to rest. I do wonder, though, how the draft board would have solved the dilemma if it weren't for the pregnancy.

One perk seldom mentioned about being in government service was the reduced cost of transportation. With a uniform on, hitchhiking anywhere was easy. All one had to do was stand at the side of the road and put out your thumb. You'd have a ride in no time. It was unpatriotic not to pick up a serviceman by the side of the road. Often the driver would go out of his way to get you to your destination, using up his gas allocation for a good cause. I made many trips from Hamilton, New York to New York City to visit June during this period, and most of the time I incurred no transportation cost.

I am very grateful for the treatment I got in the Navy. I not only had my college paid for, but I learned about the diversity of people and how a democratic and sometimes inefficient government works. I was lucky to have had the experience.

MARRIAGE AND FAMILY

I first met June Chadwick when her family moved from Elizabeth, New Jersey to Hillside, two blocks from my family's home. We were grade school age and were assigned to the same class at Saybrook School. She had a brother, Walter, two years her senior. I had a brother, Bob, two years my junior. We were born within a year of each other. June also had a sister, fifteen years her junior, for whom we babysat at times.

We started dating when we were fifteen years old, juniors in high school. We were both in the school orchestra and attended many school functions together. In our senior year, we dated every Friday and Saturday night. One of our favorite Saturday night activities was roller skating to music at a local indoor rink which was within a long walk from our homes. While both families had cars, gasoline restrictions precluded the use of cars for purely social purposes and we were too young to get drivers licenses anyway.

Although I was, and still am, a poor dancer, we attended many school dances together. While World War II was raging during this period, it was an otherwise happy time for both of us. Relaxed and unassuming, June was winsome. She finished second in the "Cutest" category in the "Senior Superlatives" voting which was part of our yearbook.

We never discussed "going steady". We just did it.

While I was in college and in the Navy, we wrote to each other at least once a week. There were, of course, no cell phones, email, texting, or other communication devices which are available now.

I graduated from Colgate University, was commissioned an ensign in the Navy and was released to inactive duty in May 1946 – all within one hectic week.

I spent that summer deciding what to do next. I applied to Harvard Graduate School of Business and to Columbia Graduate School of Journalism. With huge post-war applications, I was deferred by both schools for a year. I enrolled at New York University (NYU) Graduate School of Business, attending evening classes, and, with my father's encouragement, joined the local accounting firm of Puder and Puder as a staff accountant. Both June and I were living at home. She had a good job working for a single practitioner lawyer in Newark. Her salary was almost double mine. Neither of our parents asked for any money while we were each living at home, so we were able to save much of our income. Making enough money to become financially independent was a higher priority than waiting a year to attend either Harvard or Columbia.

In late 1946, I had saved enough money to buy an engagement ring. We visited the store of a jeweler client of June's employer, and I, on one memorable lunch hour spent my entire net worth (small as it was) on a ring. How many men can boast that they spent all their accumulated wealth on an engagement ring! Anyway, we were both happy about the transaction. June still wears the ring.

June Chadwick – engagement picture, 1946

Photo: Walter T. Cocker, Elizabeth, N.J.

June's parents hosted an engagement dinner at their home soon after. My mother, whose health was slowly deteriorating, made a great effort to attend. She was worried that we were too young to be married and that religious differences might be a difficulty in the marriage. Her concerns turned out to be of no consequence. We planned to be married within a year, but my mother's death in the summer of 1947 led to a postponement of the wedding date until April 1948.

We had a small wedding ceremony at June's church in Hillside, and a large dinner reception at the inappropriately named Freedom Room in the Douglas Hotel in Newark, which is long gone. June's little sister, Judy, played a piano solo and was a flower girl.

We borrowed my family's Nash car and drove to Miami Beach for our honeymoon where we stayed gratis at an ocean front motel. We mostly ate in fast food restaurants and our recreational spending, during our one week's stay, consisted of attending the Miami Minor League baseball team's home games. Upon reflection, I don't think June enjoyed this activity as much as I did, but she didn't complain.

Upon returning from our honeymoon, we went to live in a one room, one bath apartment in Newark. At the time, there was a huge shortage of apartments. No new construction had been developed during the war and young people, like us, all wanted to get married and start out on their own.

Fortunately, one of my father's partners owned a small apartment building in East Orange, New Jersey and we were soon able to move into this facility.

New cars were in great demand, and we had to wait a year to buy one, relying on public transportation. Eventually, we were able to purchase a new car for cash, a Studebaker. Again, much of our now combined net income went into the auto purchase.

One of our first uses of the new car was for me to teach June to drive. She learned quickly, practicing each day after work, and got her license soon thereafter.

We spent very little on entertainment during our first years of marriage, visiting family, including my grandparents in Newark many Friday evenings. We did take short vacations to New England in each of the first two years of marriage, usually with our also newly married friends, Jane and Warren Totten. Warren had grown up with us in Hillside. Our mothers had been church-related social friends since 1929, and we have been close friends ever since. Warren had been fortunate, having won a new car in a raffle, and we put many miles on that car together.

Lifelong friends, Jane and Warren Totten

In order to function as an accountant, I had to take many finance courses at NYU as quickly as I could, and I took the Port Authority Trans-Hudson (PATH) train from Newark to lower Manhattan three times a week after work to learn as quickly as I could. It worked for me. I soon become an employee who knew what he was doing and I was able to pass the CPA exam before graduating with a Master's Degree in Business Administration.

During this period, my father remarried, to the nurse who had helped my mother during her final year. Peg Mitchell was a widow with two children the same ages as my brother and me. It was a very successful marriage which lasted until my father's death in 1982.

Neither June nor I had been brought up living in apartments and we both wanted to buy a house as soon as possible and start a family. We saved as much money as we could and, without doing much shopping around, purchased a small, new Cape Cod house in Madison, New Jersey. The price was $13,000 and again we depleted our entire cash reserves, depositing $3,000 and signing a $10,000, four percent Government Issue (GI) mortgage which we worried about paying. Neither of us had ever incurred debt before, and we were scared. We couldn't foresee that inflation would help us out. We sold that house four years later at a thirty percent profit and built a new home in Madison, which is still our primary residence.

Madison was a good choice for us. Many newly formed young families like us were building their homes much like ours. Everything was booming – construction, churches, social events, community activities. A couples club was formed at the Madison Presbyterian Church which held a monthly dinner and amateur entertainment put on by a committee of members. The church hall could accommodate 240 people, and each month, invitations were sent out to the club members, arriving in Friday's mail. By Saturday noon, that month's dinner was sold out. Each committee was established six months in advance of the dinner for which they were responsible. There was a fixed, rather low price, and each committee was required to plan to break even financially.

This same church had a Sunday school with a dozen classrooms, served by more than fifty volunteer teachers in two fully-attended sessions each Sunday. This church activity is just one example of the vibrancy which the young families brought to Madison.

Now that we owned a home, we naturally decided to start our own family. My career was developing nicely, and we decided we'd have enough income if June were to be a full-time mother. At that time, this was the usual path which young families followed.

Few women followed careers, and eagerly became full-time devoted mothers, although most of the young mothers we knew had good educations and the potential to succeed in a variety of careers. All this has changed, of course. In my view, the decision to continue a full-time career after becoming a mother is a very personal and often difficult one. It's a complicated subject, one I'm not comfortable in discussing, since I have no thoughtful answer, only my own experiences to relate to. My own children and their spouses have each approached this issue in various ways, and I think they have been very successful in raising their families. All I can say is that balancing family, careers and community service needs constant vigilance and reappraisal as one goes through the process, and what works in one set of circumstances does not automatically apply in others.

June and I never decided on how many children we might have. We just had them, although when we got to four, we knew it was enough.

Frederick Richard Rohn (Rick), our oldest, was a very easy going baby. He slept when he was supposed to, ate when he was supposed to, was always happy, and seldom cried. A piece of cake, we thought, this parenthood.

Then, fifteen months later, Kathy joined us. She slept in the daytime, stayed awake at night, ate sporadically, and cried often. Sixty years later, she is still a "night person." At the time, we worried where we had gone wrong with Kathy. The answer, of course, was that we had done nothing wrong. Kathy just had a different personality than Rick.

By the time Douglas, and then Barbara were born, we had better determined what parenthood was all about. While you can get good advice from grandparents, you learn best from applying your instincts to the various challenges being a parent presents to you. We've made some mistakes, none of them major, fortunately, and, all in all, June and I are proud of successfully raising a family, the most important activity of our lives.

Our children. From left, Kathy, Douglas, Barbara and Rick

Our four children are both similar in some ways and diverse in others. Each is highly educated with advanced degrees. Each has excelled in the liberal arts, but each also has an interest, and some flair for the business world. Each married educated mates with their own career choices.

Comparing one's children with each other is not a good idea and I shall refrain from doing so. Instead, I'll just summarize their individualities without suggesting that a trait defined for one does not mean it is lacking in the others.

Rick is disciplined, detail-oriented, goal-oriented, and has developed patience over the years. He tends to be a workaholic. His decisions are based upon rational thought, not particularly influenced by emotion. His talents dovetail into his career as a legal litigator.

Kathy, in many ways is just the opposite. Her ability to communicate is a most impressive attribute. She also has the capacity to evaluate people and situations from an emotional standpoint, but come to conclusions based upon hard facts. Her knowledge of media and production adds substantially to her reservoir of abilities.

Doug's strength is relating to and managing people. He has learned to be highly organized and combines hard facts and emotional reactions to good advantage. He is good under pressure in business. His executive role in a large corporate environment, is in my view, a perfect situation for him.

Barbara is more like her brother Rick in many ways. She, with husband, Mike Vitelli, made the difficult choice of putting aside a potential business career to raise four boys. She's still at it, but now has some time for other business endeavors. Her "Book Club Mom" blog with a fast-growing readership is just a start.

Each of our children has gained from their respectful spouses, who in each instance has supported their individual efforts and personalities without diminishing the other person's own goals. Each has been a caring, involved parent, and each shows compassion for his or her fellow man. June and I could not ask for finer sons and daughters-in-law.

The years our children were growing up passed very quickly, filled with the usual activities consistent with a growing family. My father and Peg bought a home around the corner from us in Madison, and June's parents built a new home in New Providence, fifteen minutes from Madison. We all enjoyed the closeness which this afforded, and our children delighted in developing happy relationships with their grandparents.

All our children attended public schools in Madison, although Kathy attended the Kent Place School in Summit, New Jersey during her high school years. When it came time for college, each was well-prepared.

During these busy years, June and I continued a hectic schedule of school activities, church, social, and business functions (I actually wore out a tuxedo over one stretch of business-oriented charitable functions). My career required long hours, but I found time for charitable work, presiding as president of the Madison Area YMCA for many years.

Soon after moving to Madison, we purchased a building lot and then, with three children at the time, constructed a larger house thereon and moved into what is still our home. Later on we did add another bedroom, bath and large family room, so that we had adequate living space.

Holidays were spent with family. My father, for years, hosted a family picnic on Memorial Day for all the Rohns living in the area.

Our summers were spent in rented houses at the New Jersey shore, primarily Lavallette, where all four of our children took sailing lessons, raced small boats on Barnegat Bay and learned how to care for their boats, which frequently had mishaps. They also learned good sportsmanship, how to win and lose gracefully, how to remain calm under pressure, and understood that winning wasn't always everything. The Lavallette Yacht Club was an integral part of our family life over many years and we cherish the memories.

One fortunate financial event shaped our ability to afford college costs for our children. A friend of mine and I were able to finance a management buyout of a small advertising agency in New York City – the D.R. Group – which was a major player in direct response advertising program creations. Management eventually bought us out, providing June and me with sufficient funding for four college educations, including graduate studies. For several years, our biggest costs were payments to Colgate University. The D.R. Group investment was outstanding as were the college educations our children enjoyed.

Additionally, both Rick and Doug met girls at college whom they married. Our family has the advantage in that they we all knew these girls when they were still teenagers and have watched with pride as their lives have matured.

I'm not certain when the period of raising a family ends, but I think it may be when they are all married and on their own. This occurred gradually to us, since the marriages spanned a number of years. When asked what has been the happiest time of my life, I can, after considerable thought, say that it was the years we raised our family.

A FORTUNATE LIFE 79

Rick and family, 1997

From left: Michael, Rick, Fran and David

Pam Hesler and Associates Photography

Kathy and family, 1997

Back: Yvon and Kristina; Front: Kathy and Katie

Pam Hesler and Associates Photography

Doug and family, 1997

From left: Nancy, Doug and Matthew

Pam Hesler and Associates Photography

Barbara and family, 2004

Back: Barbara and Mike; Front, from left:

Gannon, Austin, Braden and Darien

Our family in 1997

Pam Hesler and Associates Photography

A FORTUNATE LIFE 83

Our family in 2004

Pam Hesler and Associates Photography

Fred and June's 90th birthday brunch, 2016

Standing: Rick, Yvon, Doug, Nancy and Mike

Seated: Fran, Kathy, June, Fred and Barbara

Wedding Day: Kristina and Ethan, 2011

Wedding Day: Michael and Mikaela, 2015

Caribbean cruise with family

Standing: Fred, Dick and Bob

Seated: June, Janet and Joan

Fred and June, 2004

Pam Hesler and Associates Photography

Fred's 80th birthday celebration, Gettysburg, PA, 2006

June and Fred, best friends

GRANDCHILDREN

Nine grandchildren is just the right number, from a grandparent's perspective. Nine is too many to dote upon, but not so many one cannot, with some effort, stay current with the ongoing activities of each. Being a part of their lives adds to a grandparent's own life, and hopefully, enhances each grandchild's life as well.

All grandparents think of their grandchildren in glowing terms, and I'm no exception. I try to be objective about them, but it is a difficult process.

Five of my grandchildren grew up in cities: New York, Washington and Brussels. All five, primarily because they lived in cities, attended private schools. The seven who have gone to college have attended seven different schools – so far. They all have been fortunate in being provided with these educational activities. They all have many cousins who can add to the quality of total family life. I had only four cousins, and we seldom socialized, even though we lived reasonably close to each other. Perhaps we each missed something.

I want to say something about each grandchild individually. This is a bit tricky. It is important to avoid comparisons which could stir up rivalries among them and their parents.

There are many similarities among them. All are career-oriented, thrive on education, have good communication skills, and have compassionate natures. Their parents have done excellent jobs in raising them.

Each grandchild is special in his or her own way, and are joys to watch grow into adulthood. They cannot yet fully appreciate how important they are to their grandparents. The priorities of their expanding lives provide them with little time for reflection on their relationships with grandparents. We can only hope that they will remain closely bound to each other, to their parents, and have fond memories of their grandparents.

65th wedding anniversary celebration with our children and grandchildren, 2013

Here's what I'd like to say about each of them:

Kristina: Happily married to Ethan, who is completing his medical doctor's internship, Kristina is employed in a museum environment which provides the starting basis for a career in management of non-profit organizations. Compassion, thoughtfulness and kindness are strengths in her character.

Michael: Also happily married, to Mikaela, a hard-working attorney, Michael has embarked on an interesting career path which includes assisting candidates for office with fundraising and other services. He is good with people, considerate, ambitious yet laid back. He could expand his service to candidates in speech writing, polling, interviewing and other services politicians require if he wants to. He'll figure this out for himself.

<u>Katie</u>: Katie possesses many skills and has multiple interests, including her background in photography, media and an increasing interest in the business and financial world. Ambitious and resolute, Katie is poised for success in life. It's an improbable, but not idle thought, that she and Michael, with complementary skills and interests, would be good business partners.

<u>David</u>: David's outstanding affinity in relating to young people, and his love of sports, has led him to launch a career that capitalizes on these two attributes. He will be an effective leader as he gains experience.

<u>Matthew</u>: Matt is the only one of our nine grandchildren with a deep interest in science. Affable, warm and articulate, he will be an excellent doctor after he completes his medical school education. My guess is that he will also be a good businessman.

Austin: Sports journalism is his passion, and he is an excellent reporter with good writing skills. Austin is focused on the future, is a superior college student and is confident about himself and his future. He's chosen a career which will utilize his talents to their fullest.

Darien: As a college student majoring in economics, Darien has shown an interest in the business world, a very broad category of a career path. His self-confidence will enable him to forge a place in the business world which will lead him to success. He's aiming toward a degree in finance.

Gannon: College lies ahead for Gannon a year from now. It's too early to tell the direction of his career and life, but he's off to a good start. The older brothers setting an example is very helpful. Gannon has shown a keen interest in communications and sports management.

Braden: As a young teenager, Braden continues to develop new interests. A good listener, he absorbs knowledge, and tries out ideas that he creates. Braden is developing skills which are quite different than his brothers and cousins, and it will be interesting to watch these attributes grow.

So, that's a short synopsis of our grandchildren. We're obviously proud of each of them, are delighted that they are healthy, positive thinking young people who have, fortunately, caring parents, great educations and opportunities which many others their ages do not enjoy. They have, as the saying goes, "everything going for them."

How should a grandfather fit into the lives of nine vibrant lives? Here are my roles.

1. Don't criticize. If you don't approve of some action on their part, keep it to yourself, unless your view is sought.
2. Don't usurp, or interfere with the guidance of your grandchildren's parents. You're not in charge.
3. Don't give advice unless asked.
4. Treat each grandchild as unique, but also equally. Foster one-on-one relationships. Sometimes grandchildren will tell you things about their lives which they are uncomfortable telling their parents, using you as a conduit. This should be a plus and doesn't undermine the parent-child relationship.

I have found these rules relatively easy to follow, and that they work in enhancing togetherness with the family.

Finally, what advice would I give to my grandchildren? Only a few ideas seem appropriate. They each have their own lives to lead, decisions to make. Here's all that I will say.

1) Communicate with others. Each of you has the skill set to transmit facts, emotions, and reactions.
2) Attempt to separate emotional response from logical analysis. It may be desirable at times to act out of emotion, but you should understand the logic of the situation involved before reacting.
3) Don't succumb, or try to avoid, the pressures of any situation. Tension is integral to all activities. Learn how to live with it.

Each of these suggestions requires discipline to implement, but I think is well worth the effort.

Much of what is discussed in this chapter focuses on education and careers. These are important elements in living a happy, productive life. But add to these aspects, good health, a positive attitude and good fortune, and you are destined to achieve a meaningful life.

FRIENDS

We all have social, business, school, neighborhood affinity groups, political and other friendships, often overlapping among the categories. Some have developed and matured over a lifetime, others are a more recent vintage. I'm not recalling anything new here, but I think it may be interesting to learn what friendships have meant to me. Of course, June is, and has throughout my life, been my very best friend.

I have found that, over a lifetime, the best friends are those I've known the longest, sometimes more than fifty years. Over time, I've interacted with friends at many levels, at different ages, in various situations. I have seen others at their and my best, and our worst. I know others' strengths and faults. I can be irked by these friends as well as be uplifted by them. I can predict their reactions, and count on their support under any circumstances. Ideally, these friends, of both June's and mine, are often married couples, and the best relationships rely on mutual emotional connections and compatibility with each other. June and I have a very few friends who fit into this category. They are a treasure to us. It's probably a good idea not to identify them for fear of inadvertently leaving out some names, or embarrassing them for having been singled out.

As the lives of friends have ended, we have developed a number of new friends. This replenishing process is essential to our overall quality of life. It's one of the important virtues of being a senior citizen. We miss our departed friends and the fond memories we have shared. Our new friends cannot replace the old ones, but they do contribute to the fullness of our lives.

June and I have been fortunate to have an established group of friends who have added depth, stimulation, emotional support, and hopefully, to whom we have added to the quality of their lives. Just for the fun of it, I've listed ten well-known people whom I'd have liked to have called friends. Some are living, others have departed this world, but all have lived during my lifetime. I'm not certain how much my friendship might have meant to them, but I would have worked hard at being meaningful to them at some emotional level of friendship. The list is somewhat eclectic, but perhaps suggests that a diversity of friendships is one I have always desired. Here they are:

1. <u>Jimmy Carter</u>. Perhaps not the best overall president of our nation, Jimmy Carter has spent more than three decades of his post-presidency, serving to help solve some of the world's knottiest problems. His compassion, steadfastness, respect for mankind, and deeply religious nature, are inspirational. He and I are the same age (some say we even look alike) and I know we could have been good, personal friends, if our paths in life had crossed.

2. <u>Eleanor Roosevelt</u>. Her devotion to improving the lives of each of us, propelled by a resolute energy, was highly inspirational for me.

3. <u>Martin Luther King, Jr</u>. Dr. King's passionate yet calming nature has been a symbol of the slow march to freedom to an oppressed people of color. He championed a major shift of thinking in this country and could have taught me much on how to take hold of a complicated subject and break it down to build a simple, understandable plan for positive action.

4. <u>Thomas Edison</u>. With an inquisitive mind, and a patient investigative approach to experimentation, he changed

many ways in which we live. As a mentor, he could have challenged me to more often "think outside the box."

5. <u>Barack Obama</u>. It's too soon to tell, but Obama may go down in history as one of our greater presidents. Certainly, his compassion, intellect, confidence and patience have served him well. What he accomplishes in his post-presidency will be revealing.

6. <u>Yogi Berra</u>. Humble, passionate, an unintellectual intellectual, Yogi turned a storied baseball career into a source of inspiration for everyone. How could you not want to be the friend of this wonderful man!

7. <u>Harry Truman</u>. Another humble, non-intellectual, yet determined and logical thinker, Truman made what may have been the most important decision of the last one hundred years – the implementation of the atom bomb. Accounting for killing more than 200,000 people in order to save millions more was daunting, yet he made the world-changing decision fearlessly.

8. <u>Jack Paar</u>. The late night show pioneer based his interviews on intellectual byplay, bringing out the best in his guests so that we got to know them. Silly jokes seldom found their way into this TV show.

9. <u>Albert Einstein</u>. Self-effacing with an intellect too great to shape easily with the less inspired, I would have liked to talk to him about sailing, food and other day-to-day pleasures. He never tried to capitalize on his discoveries. That is a refreshing attribute.

10. <u>Bill Gates</u>. Gates made a fortune from his ideas and has now put that fortune to work to help make the world a better place. What could be a more American Horatio Alger story? I'd like to discuss with him how he measures the effectiveness of his current endeavors.

There are others I could name, but these will suffice, although I might add Sandra Day O'Connor to the list. The reader may discover something about me from my creating this list that might otherwise not be evident. That's one purpose of a personal memoir.

The bottom line on this chapter is to emphasize how important friendships are to me. I don't think I've ever told a friend how much he or she has meant to me. Hopefully, this chapter, even without names, will remedy my error.

CAREER CHOICES

Young people, at least most of them, devote a good amount of time to planning what they might best do with their lives, given their talents and circumstances. Education, of course, is the starting point in this process. Here's what I think about education.

College is a privilege and should be available to all. Hopefully that day will come.

For purposes of this discussion, I am going to assume that the high school student wants to go to college to expand his or her mind and skills, and has the financial capacity either through family, scholarships, and/or student loans to make attending college possible. This may not be a typical situation throughout our country, but our immediate family is fortunate enough so that college attendance is a given. Hopefully, all our family members appreciate how lucky they have been, or are.

So, the question becomes – what kind of college education do I want, and where can I best get it?

Few high school students have fully developed ideas on what kind of work they want to do. For those who don't know what they want to do, my experience has provided me with a strong feeling that a liberal arts college education is a preferable college path to follow. I recognize that a liberal arts education is a luxury in itself, and doesn't provide identifiable job opportunities. Many liberal arts college graduates find they need to obtain further, specialized education, another luxury, both financially and timewise. But if they follow this route, they are likely to have enhanced skills, primarily in the ability to communicate, which will serve them well in whatever career they may follow. Let me provide an example.

My own undergraduate degree was in English and creative writing. And then, following my father's footsteps, I became an accountant, eventually secured a graduate degree in accounting and became a partner in a large public accounting firm. One doesn't think of accounting as requiring writing skills, and most accountants obtain business degrees which do not stress the development of writing skills. To the best of my knowledge, I was the only partner with an undergraduate degree which included creative writing. This background provides me with training which allowed me to write reports, including footnotes to financial statements with more clarity than many of my peers. When one considers the fact that typical financial reports normally consist of three pages of financial data and as much as fifty pages of detailed footnotes, it is easy to see why communication skills are important. My daughter Kathy, without any formal training in accounting, has forged a second career working with the highly intelligent accounting trained staff of one of the nation's largest accounting firms, in providing written and oral clarity in their proposals, reports and public relations.

Most career vocations are enhanced by applying polished writing and speaking skills. Lawyers write briefs and argue cases. Teachers lecture their students, politicians give speeches in attempts to influence their constituencies, and managers write memos to motivate their staffs. One can go on, job by job, profession by profession, illustrating how communication skills, the backbone of liberal arts education, positively influence job performance.

My children and grandchildren have all followed this path, and it has, and will help them, not only in their careers, but in communicating with whom they come in contact with throughout their lives.

I don't believe it matters much where one goes to college, as long as the student is happy and motivated. A school which fosters diversity in its student body is a major benefit since interfacing with individuals with dissimilar backgrounds helps prepare students for the globalization which is transforming our world.

All this education takes time and energy. At times the process can be drudgery, but it is worth it if you can make it happen.

Now, for the easier part. Once you have the education, take whatever job interests you and pays your current bills. I thought I'd like to be a journalist after graduating from college. Instead I took a job in accounting. It didn't matter that those two career paths had little in common on the surface.

But communication skills are vital in both. I have never regretted my choice of professions. Usually the same basic talents and skills provide you for success in a variety of professions and you can be happy, satisfied, content and thus successful even if, through circumstances you drift into a career that you never had considered.

I want to conclude this chapter with the following caveat. The liberal arts path is not for everyone, and no absolute route is the only one. I can only say that, within my family, what I have described in this chapter seems to be working for us.

SPORTS

People throughout the world love sports, both participating in and watching them. Sports can be a catalyst bringing together peoples of all kinds of cultures. Professional and amateur sports organizations, as well as governments, need to devote resources to promote international inter-country sports involvement in a multitude of activities from baseball, basketball and soccer to lacrosse, field hockey and swimming, as well as others. Sports stir developments inside us and this energy can be expanded to help achieve a sense of mutual pride and togetherness among all.

I admit to loving baseball and basketball best as a participant. Like many young boys, I dreamed about being the next Lou Gehrig or Larry Bird. Also, like most boys, I wasn't good enough to achieve even a slight amount of success as a high school or college athlete. Sure, I could throw a baseball hard and with reasonable accuracy, and certainly I could get off a quick shot at the basket with some accuracy, but I grew to be only five feet, nine inches tall, with a short arm and small fingers. All the desire inside me and many years of practice made me as proficient as I could become, but didn't propel me to stardom. My dreams of sports success gradually evaporated (shattered would be too strong a word). But I was not discouraged. I kept throwing baseballs and shooting baskets at every opportunity, in my back yard where my father had installed a basketball hoop on the garage door, and on the playgrounds.

My mother was not into sports. She viewed high school teams as a distraction from school work, and therefore something to be avoided. My father said nothing. So I didn't play on high school sports teams. My mother relented at the beginning of my high school senior year and said I could play basketball. Easy for her to say, I thought. You don't start as a member of the team as a senior. But I persevered and I asked the coach, Al Vreeland, if I could join the team. I pointed out that I thought I was good enough to be on the team. In fact, I said I thought I was better than a couple seniors who were on the team. Al Vreeland knew my abilities from gym class which he taught and said to me, "You want me to replace someone on the team who has been working hard for three years to be part of it. I can't do that, there are just so many kids allowed on a team, and I'm not throwing a senior off the squad who has been with the program for three years. I'm sorry."

I felt bad about this at the time, but I never got angry with my mother. She acted in accordance with her own view of sports. She did realize, I am sure, that her position was in the minority. My life wasn't ruined, and maybe her decision did help my studies. I like to think that I could have handled both school work and team sports simultaneously.

With a few other non-varsity basketball players, I formed a team that played pick-up games whenever and wherever we could. We had no coach, just figured out how to use our individual skills to good advantage. The high school varsity team was mediocre, and we suggested to Coach Vreeland that our little team play the varsity as a fundraiser for the senior class. I was certain we could beat them. Coach Vreeland turned us down, citing scholastic rules that prohibited such events. Looking back, I'm sure he thought we might beat his varsity team. Unfortunately, Coach Vreeland, who was a good man, suffered a fatal heart attack soon after. He couldn't have been fifty years old.

The next year as a seventeen-year-old freshman at Colgate University, I tried out for the school's freshman basketball team. It wasn't much of a tryout. It was the height of the war years and there was no recruiting, so I made the team. I really wasn't very good, though, compared to the others, so I didn't get to play much. And I eventually left the team.

Possibly the most noteworthy personnel matter on the basketball team that year was the participation on the varsity team of Otto Graham, who was the star quarterback of the Cleveland Browns team in the NFL, and had been sent to Colgate for officer training. The National Collegiate Athletic Association (NCAA) prohibited professional football players from playing college football while in service, but they could play other sports. Graham was obviously a gifted athlete and had played high school basketball and then joined the Colgate varsity basketball team. The problem he had was that he had become used to the contact sport of football and he constantly fouled out of the games. I had the experience of watching his self-frustration as the referee called yet another foul on him. Playing basketball may have helped keep him in physical shape, but it certainly did nothing for his super-size athletic status. When the war ended, he returned to Cleveland and enjoyed a long highly successful football career.

My father liked sports as I did, particularly baseball. For several years growing up, we went to a game each Sunday afternoon. Occasionally my brother would join us, but most often he opted not to go. He never liked team sports as I did.

The Newark Bears were in the International League, one step below the Major Leagues. The Bears were owned by the New York Yankees who at the time were owned by Jacob Ruppert, owner of a leading brewery headquartered in Newark. We would attend many of the home games during the early and late season. (I attended camp in the Poconos in the mid-summer months.) There was always a double header. In the opening game, two teams from the Negro Major League played, and the Bears played the second game. Black and white fans mixed throughout the afternoon. I never observed any racial tension even though the teams themselves were segregated.

It was obvious to me, even as a boy, that some of the black players were better than their Newark Bears counterparts. What didn't occur to me, or to all the fans, was that the black players had reached as far in the baseball world as they could, while the white players had potential Major League Baseball opportunities.

In 1937, the Newark Bears had a very impressive roster. It was said that they could have beaten every team in the American League except the New York Yankees. The Yankees were loaded with talent – that is why the Bears were so good. There was no way to break into the Yankee roster. All the Bears players were young and gifted, except their shortstop, Nolan Richardson, who was the glue that solidified the infield. Atley Donald, Steve Bundra and Vito Tamulous were superior starting pitchers, and catcher Buddy Rosal became a Major League star. As an eleven-year-old, I tried to emulate Atley Donald's best pitch. It was called a "drop" baseball, falling several inches as it crossed home plate. Now that pitch is much more common and is labeled a "sinker." Both terms are highly descriptive. I never could master how to throw such a pitch. You need long fingers to accomplish this. If you want to understand how long fingers are a requirement in guiding a pitch from mound to plate, take a look at Satchel Paige holding a baseball.

When the Bears were not playing at home, my father and I would go to Echo Lake Park to watch the semi pro teams in action. Admission was free and a hat was passed for donations, sometimes twice during the game. My favorite team to watch were "The Sons of David." You needed a full beard to play on this team, the fuller the better. Beards made twenty-year-olds look the same as forty-year-olds, and it was often hard to tell one player from another. I never found out how or why a religious sect had a baseball team, but there was something to observe behind the beards, and that was fun to watch.

Undoubtedly, my most satisfying sports activity was managing a "Little League" group of ten to twelve-year-olds. If you can get the trust and attention of kids that age, you can accomplish wondrous things in their development as individuals. It is not an easy task. The national organization, which has developed and monitors Little League Baseball, provides managers and coaches with sound advice on the subject, but nothing is more important than patience, even-handedness, dedication, perseverance and organization. You have to show up at every practice and game on time with a lineup prepared and a cheerleading talk ready. More than once, over the five years I was a Little League manager, did I have to excuse myself from a business meeting in order to get to a Little League game or practice.

The team I managed was sponsored by Al's Sport Shop, a local establishment which competed successfully with the large chains selling athletic gear. Our success as a team which resulted in weekly newspaper articles, was great. Publicity for Al's Sport Shop and was well worth the cost of sponsorship.

My team was newly formed when I became manager, one of two new teams added to our town's complement of what had been a six-team league.

My first duty was to pick fourteen players from analyzing a pool of boys who wanted to play. The other new team manager and I were each allotted six choices and then all eight teams would draft players one after the other to complete their rosters. There was a Saturday morning tryout at which all those aspiring to play in the Little League would bat and field in order to impress the attending managers and coaches.

My son Doug was ten years old at the time. He knew a lot of the boys – who was good and who wasn't. He also told me that the best recruits were pretty well known to the other managers and had been told they didn't have to excel at the tryouts. Doug gave me a list of who he thought were the best ten and eleven-year-olds, and I followed his suggestions. As a result, we had a nucleus of good young baseball players which propelled us to a dominant position over the following three years. Although I didn't know it at the time, I later found out that the other managers, most of whom had been managing for many years, were impressed by our ability to draft players, and we gained their respect.

One of the challenges managers often face is interference from team members' parents. Usually the interference had to do with playing time. I followed a formula in using the players without deviation and never had any arguments from parents. My best five players would play the entire game unless we were far ahead in the scores, and the rest of the team would each play an equal number of innings. This formula was well within the league rules.

I developed many interesting relationships with my team members over the years. For a short time, I was the most important person in their lives, excluding parents. To this day, some fifty years later, former players go out of their way to greet me in town. I don't often recognize them, but they know me. It's a good feeling.

I'll end this discussion about Little League baseball with one poignant story. In my first year as manager, one ten-year-old came to me and said he didn't have a baseball glove, that his mother (no father was mentioned) couldn't afford one, and that he knew that the rules stated that every player must have and maintain his own glove. What should he do?

I bought him a glove and he proudly used it during the next two games. The next week, he approached me and said he had lost his glove, intimating that someone had stolen it. I arranged for him to borrow one of his teammate's gloves for the next game. I purchased another glove for him and admonished him to be more careful.

A couple of weeks went by and he again came to me and said his newest glove had disappeared also. I told him I wasn't buying him any more gloves and that he'd have to borrow a glove from a teammate from now on.

At the next game, when it was time for him to enter the game, he told me he couldn't play because no one would lend him a glove. I checked and found this to be true. What I didn't know until the next day, when one of the boys tipped me off, was that the gloveless boy had sold both of the gloves which I had purchased for him. Without a glove, he couldn't play and sat out a couple of games before the other team members relented and let him borrow their gloves.

I'm still not sure how I should have reacted to this episode. I don't know whether his family needed the money or whether he was just being opportunistically immoral. I decided not to do or say anything. Hopefully, the peer pressure expended by the other members of the team in not lending him a glove for a period of time, taught him a lesson. As I recall, the following year he had his own glove which he used throughout the season.

I feel compelled to make a comment about physical violence in sports, particularly football and boxing. I must admit there is some enjoyment gleaned from watching a display of brute force against brute force, but the potential incapacities which too often negatively affect athletes in these physically combative sports diminishes their appeal to me. I prefer watching the application of skill over hitting one's opponent as hard as possible. That's why I like baseball so much. The most physical of plays, the home plate collision, has been banned, and a player can go through a 162-game schedule without physical contact with another player except for a base-stealing tag or the slide to break up a potential double play. I am glad that none of my grandsons played high school or college football or took up boxing. They will be glad they didn't when they are ninety years old.

When you're young, participating in sports helps develop the body and provides each of us with an understanding of our own body, what it can accomplish, and how it can perform in relation to others. As a spectator, sports provides, as does music, both a stimulus and a sedative to mind and emotion.

MUSIC

I grew up in an era of fifteen member "swing" bands, in the years between World War I and World War II. Dixieland later evolved and broadened, recording techniques improved and musicians welcomed a new revenue source through sale of records.

There were many dance bands that played in "supper clubs" which were really restaurants with large stages and dance floors. Bands would be booked for two-week gigs and then would move on to another location. In New Jersey, Frank Daly's Meadowbrook on Route 23 in Pompton Plains was nationally known. In New York, the most popular venue was the Glen Island Casino. All the well-known big bands played in each of these locations and radio broadcasts of live dance sets were common.

I liked orchestral music. I, with parental insistence, had taken many years of piano lessons and was good enough so that I got the job of pianist in my high school during my junior and senior years. I was fascinated how the combined sounds of strings, horns and woodwinds were blended into smooth melodic sequences, unified by a steady, sometimes dominating drum beat. I would have loved to have become an arranger, but the opportunity to learn how never presented itself. I'm not sure I'd consider this a regret, but it would have been a career, or at least an avocation, I would have enjoyed.

The best known big bands included Benny Goodman, Harry James, Artie Shaw, Ray McKinley, Woody Herman, Count Basie, Duke Ellington and the Dorsey Brothers. But my favorites were Glenn Miller and Louis Prima. Glenn Miller's arrangement, built around a clarinet and tenor saxophone, created a smooth tone which no other band could duplicate. The band's theme song, "Moonlight Serenade" was a perfect blend of woodwinds and horns. His band could play slow, sweet ballads, or upbeat tempos such as "Chattanooga Choo Cho" and "I've Got a Gal in Kalamazoo." Both of these latter two songs had catchy lyrics, enhanced by the distinctive vocals of Tex Benecke.

Some of the songs these bands played were what at the time were considered "corny" and often the band leaders lacked personality and showmanship. Miller, the Dorseys, James and

Goodman, highly professional though they were, did not project a warmth of personality themselves, leaving their music to be the entire entertainment. Count Basie, Artie Shaw, Woody Herman, Cab Calloway and Duke Ellington were better at showmanship.

But my favorite, from a showmanship standpoint, was Louis Prima. He was a good musician flaunting a very professional band, but he always seemed to be making fun of his efforts. Possessing a gravelly voice, constantly prancing around the podium, and aided and abetted by his lead saxophonist, Sam Butera, and his young wife, Keely Smith, he turned otherwise unremarkable songs into pure entertainment. "I Ain't Got Nobody," "Hey Babe, Hey Girl," "Hey Marie," and "When You're Smiling" are masterpieces. Throughout these songs, Keely Smith stood quietly alongside her ever-moving husband with a look of disdain and boredom and beneath that veneer, a completely befuddled yet mocking attitude. Once in a while she'd copy, awkwardly, one of Prima's outrageous prancing dance steps, always with a blank look on her face. "What are you doing, you fool, Louis?" she seemed to be saying. None of this was obviously evident on records, but seeing this band in person was a unique treat. Keely Smith's voice is among the rarest of one hundred singers I have heard, and she is my all-time favorite.

There are other great female singers I have enjoyed, including Billie Holiday, Ella Fitzgerald, Sarah Vaughn, Eydie Gorme and Jo Stafford. All had perfect pitch, intuitive phrasing and the ability to project a song to the audience. There were many female band singers who were good, but to me they were as a group unremarkable.

As for male big band and solo singers, Bing Crosby and Frank Sinatra were the most popular. But my favorites were Mel Tormé, Bobby Darrin and Tony Bennett. Tormé's "The Christmas Song", Darrin's, "Mack the Knife" and "Beyond the Sea" and Bennett's "San Francisco" are my all-time favorites. I also love the unusual sound and projection which makes Rod Stewart special.

There were many excellent musicians forming the Big Bands. In addition to Benny Goodman and Artie Shaw, who were clarinet virtuosos, Woody Herman, Jimmy Dorsey and later, Pete Fountain, were outstanding. Harry James's trumpet solos of "Flight of the Bumble Bee" and "Ciribiribin" are breathtaking. Tommy Dorsey's solo in "I'm in a Sentimental Mood" is moving. Woody Herman's "Woodchoppers Ball" is show-stopping.

Gas rationing during World War II forced the closing of the supper club venues and the bands played in smaller, downtown locations, close to bus and trolley mass transit. It was both illegal and unpatriotic to drive a car just to hear a band, even if you had some gasoline coupons unused. So, my friends and I, often in my high school years, would take a bus on Saturday mornings to Newark where the Adams Theater on Branford Place housed a succession of big bands in concert. For some reason, this wasn't a boy/girl dating pursuit. I always went with boys only.

I found that there was more listening than dancing to Big Band music. The exception was those of us who liked to "Jitterbug" which didn't include me. "Jitterbugging" was a craze at the time, fueled by Mickey Rooney's "Andy Hardy" movies. Mickey, with help from Judy Garland, usually, as high schoolers would suggest, at the movie's start, that the school put on a show. Usually, there would be a Jitterbug contest which he would win. He was a good dancer, and many high school contemporaries copied his athletic moves and the dance bands always played a set or two of fast-paced musical numbers for the benefit of these dancers.

Offsetting the upbeat Jitterbug tempos, many of the songs were slowly played ballads, conducive to encourage teens with limited dancing skills to huddle closely, two-by-two, and move slowly to the rhythms.

Some ingenious music arrangers figured out how to portray a song with an upbeat tempo, suitable for Jitterbugging, but at the same time creating an atmosphere fitting for slow dancing. Somehow, Louis Prima could often accomplish this dual presentation. Tempo had much to do with it, including drumming. I never figured out the secret to this.

Probably my most memorable Big Band experience took place after June's and my Junior/Senior prom in January 1942. Frank Daily had closed down his Meadowbrook Club and was opening a new venue in downtown Newark, The Terrace Room, which had been a hotel ballroom.

Our prom was scheduled for the same night as the opening, and somehow two other couples and June and I had acquired reservations to a sold out performance featuring Jimmy Dorsey. We made an appearance at the high school where the dance was being held, and then took a bus (the girls were in gowns, we boys in suits and ties) to Newark. It turned out that we had up-front seats. We stayed until the last set was over and then took a bus back home. Most of those in attendance were of drinking age, but the two Cokes we each drank were the only additional costs we incurred.

I think our total bill was seventeen dollars. We were treated with respect and were never hassled.

Bob Eberly was the male singer soloist for Jimmy Dorsey. It was before the time that he and Helen O'Connell teamed on a duet which became a big hit – "Green Eyes" – which effectively went from one slow ballad verse to a very upbeat tempo in the second verse. Helen O'Connell wasn't the female vocalist that night, and a new singer, Kitty Kallen, was making her debut with the Dorsey orchestra. She was only around three years older than each of our group, and was obviously a bit nervous. Bob Eberly was continually supportive, and she did admirably.

When I was a senior in high school, I discovered that one could purchase band orchestrations, either full-size, fifteen member ones or versions for smaller groups.

I got together six of my friends and we purchased an orchestral arrangement of a hit song at the time, "My Prayer." It had parts for piano, saxophone, clarinet, trumpet, trombone and drums. We each studied our respective parts and then did some rehearsing in my friend, Norman Govette's home basement. We joked that we'd advertise for female singer tryouts which we thought would be fun. We never did get to hold the tryouts.

When we thought we were ready to record our version of "My Prayer," Norman's father set up the recording apparatus for us and we went to work. The end result was musically flawless, but the tempo, slow enough as this ballad was anyway, was about half the speed it should have been. We were so concerned about getting the notes right that we failed to consider that we were performing a dance tune. Instead "My Prayer" became mournful. We obviously would need a lot more practice, a drummer who would lead rather than follow, and a leader who could take charge of the entire presentation.

We made a few more efforts to speed things up, but we never got there. So ended my dance band endeavor.

I couldn't discuss music without mentioning my favorite pianist, Erroll Garner. He didn't arrive on the music scene until after World War II, but since then his records, tapes and videos have been a recurring joy for me. He's best known, of course, for his composition "Misty," but his unique doubling of melodic notes on many well-known songs is enthralling.

Swing music, as promulgated by the Big Band era, has faded as new forms of music and prolific delivery systems have taken hold. Big bands still attract a following in retirement areas and occasionally I get to hear some of the old orchestrations, played convincingly by those my grandchildren's age. I'm still comforted by this music, at times in awe of its ability to get the best out of both the instruments themselves and the musicians playing together as a team. It is my kind of music, an integral part of growing up during the mid-twentieth century.

COMMUNITY SERVICE

It may seem unusual that an entire chapter be devoted to community service in a personal memoir. But as I look back upon my life, I have recognized that I devoted a good bit of energy and, in some cases, some financial support to various community services. These have been a very varied group of activities, and in reviewing them, I have asked myself why I contributed so much work to them.

Perhaps, if I itemize each activity, my reasons for understanding the efforts and my assessment of what I might have achieved, will be of some value to my grandchildren and to future generations. Each of us has the opportunity to participate, in varying degrees, in community service. To the extent one makes the effort is based on time constraints, one's abilities and the motivations which influence one getting involved. I'll try to define my own motivations and evaluate the success of the efforts from various perspectives.

It might be helpful to summarize the various reasons which motivate us to volunteer for communities. These often overlap and evolve as we pursue various activities, and I think we seldom consciously evaluate the motives in advance.

Many people feel a deep obligation to "give back to the community," especially if they are having a relatively successful life as they each define it. Society fosters this belief, and in some cases, suggests a sense of obligation to participate.

On the opposite side of human endeavor, individuals who feel cheated, or downtrodden, as the result of how the world has treated them, sometimes join efforts which are designed to correct, or at least positively change, the circumstances which have befallen them.

Some people join organizations which aim to impact a social need, such as homelessness. These participants often believe that many such problems are better dealt with by the private sector rather than government oversight and control.

One can aspire to a measure of gaining political clout by joining organizations which interface with government or with politicians or promote an activity or a particular legislative agenda.

Career enhancement might be a motivation. Does belonging to such and such an organization look good on one's resume? This may be self-serving, but has its usefulness.

Many organizations are formed to capture the interest of parents with school-age children. Supporting your children is a noble pursuit and ties directly into one's responsibility as a parent.

For retired or bored individuals, getting involved in community non-profit activities helps fill a void, creates the opportunity for new friendships, provides intellectual stimulation, makes you feel important, adds to your body of knowledge, and makes you feel, as a team member, part of something that creates positive results.

Often, involvement in community activities, is based primarily upon loyalty – to one's friends, one's school, or one's church.

And finally, social climbing is, to some, an appealing reason for joining some organizations. Under the right circumstances, such membership can provide relationships and opportunities not readily obtainable through other means. I know professional people who have built their entire professional practices on people they have met through community activities.

Of course, most organizations rely upon voluntary cash contributions in addition to volunteer work to support their efforts. My advice in this regard is to give as you are able, but don't join organizations which require a financial commitment beyond your comfort zone.

One other note of caution might be helpful. Remember that community service is an avocation, not a career in itself. The time and attention which the organization requires should be limited in time and financial support within parameters which do not sacrifice your job or your family. At its best, community involvement is an enhancement to one's job, and strengthens one's family. If too much time and attention are devoted to outside activities, the result is just the opposite.

As my life has progressed, I devoted time and attention to activities involving my children (June did the same), including baseball Little League, Parent-Teacher Association activities and YMCA organizations. I have supported Colgate University in various roles, including two terms on the Alumni Board, have contributed financially to the school's endowment as best I could, and commenced many lifelong friendships as a result. As my accounting firm's representative, I attended a couple of national conventions of the National Democratic Party and got to meet a number of political dignitaries under informal conditions.

I spent many years as a member and president twice of the New Jersey State Board of Accountancy, which licenses and monitors CPAs in New Jersey. Later, I was the lone non-engineer on the New Jersey State Board of Engineers and Land Surveyors, a role I filled for more than ten years. I have served on the board of directors of the Morris Museum, the third largest museum in New Jersey, for more than twenty years.

Morris Museum, Morristown, N.J.

My two most challenging activities were as president and board of directors member of the Madison Area YMCA and the New Jersey Historical Society. A few words about each may shed some light on the activities of these two very different organizations.

When I first became a board member of the Madison Area YMCA, we had a newly constructed facility thanks primarily to the generosity of Mrs. Horace Dodge, a long-time Madison resident and member of the Rockefeller family. It was evident that the building was too small to meet the needs of the local population, so one of our first jobs was to raise money to expand the facility. At first I was treasurer and then was elected president.

During my tenure, we completed two fund drives, added substantially to the footprint of the property and acquired a recently closed elementary school as an adjunct facility. For several years, I was at the YMCA one or two evenings a week and for a few hours on Saturdays. I worked closely with two executive directors who became lifelong friends. I don't think my career or family suffered from this commitment, and am proud of what the team of devoted volunteers contributed. Today, the YMCA is a major contributor to the local way of life and is poised for yet another fund drive and expansion. I am grateful for having been a part of an entity which has had a positive impact on life in the Madison, New Jersey area.

Madison Area YMCA, Madison, N.J.

My involvement with the New Jersey Historical Society started in an unusual manner. Mrs. Ralph Stoddard, my neighbor, who was a major YMCA supporter and from whom I purchased the lot on which our home in Madison is built, called me over to her home and insisted I get involved with the Historical Society, of which she was a longtime member. Past ninety years of age, she was very persuasive and I decided I'd better follow her strong suggestion.

It took me a couple of years to understand the organization and its constituency. The board of directors consisted of a diverse group of individuals, including some elderly, wealthy dowagers (known with affection as members of "The Far Hills Crowd"), a couple of Army old-time zealots whose mission seemed to be to promote various re-enactments of famous New Jersey battles, some professional history buffs who wanted to display the vast storehouse of artifacts which were held in a warehouse, and a couple of financial types who said we should sell a lot of our assets and get the balance sheet in shape.

Under these conditions, it was easy to become president and I was elected to that dubious office.

Our prize asset was the former governor's house, Morven, in Princeton, which had become a museum. Morven was a three bedroom house which was woefully inadequate for the use of the two governors who were the final residents of the home. Both Governor Hughes and Byrne had several children and Morven couldn't accommodate them properly, let alone serve as a functioning social headquarters.

A new future governor's home had been acquired with financing separate from the Historical Society. But there was no money available to furnish the property. The diverse board of the Historical Society now had something they could work on together. Furnish Drumthwacket!

So a fundraising effort was launched and a committee was formed to acquire the furnishings. The committee was historically focused, but impractically decided to acquire antiques to depict the various eras of New Jersey history. They ordered the furniture and had it delivered to the new facility, relying on a goodly amount of unpaid pledges to finance the acquisition.

When the new furniture was viewed in its new surroundings, no one except the committee thought well of the effort. The resounding negative reaction forced a discounted return of the furniture, the angered cancellation of unpaid pledges, and an unpaid balance due to the furniture suppliers.

The board was able to raise enough money to pay off the deficit and smooth things over with a group of well-meaning, but impractical, pure historians. I survived this episode, primarily by eliciting a sympathy vote from a number of outside sources including the governor's office. I continued for a while longer as president, and left the organization a bit more cohesive than when I joined.

N.J. Governor's Mansion, Drumthwacket, Princeton, N.J.

Photo: Virginia Hill

Earlier in this chapter, I listed various positive results emanating from community service. I can honestly say that I achieved most of the positive results I listed. I would hope that my grandchildren, and their children, might be able to do the same to the extent they are so inclined.

RELIGION

If, in defining the world religions, one were to apply the adjectives devout, fervent, zealous, pious and perhaps rigid, I would fail to meet the requirements. Yet, I do emphatically consider myself religious. I do believe in a God – a supreme being – who in some unfathomable way has produced what we wondrously know as intelligent life. I believe in the trinity of mind, body and spirit, in some form of life after death, and that the Christian faith of my upbringing is at least as good a set of principles to follow as other religions. I believe that the rigidity of various Christian and non-Christian religions has added to the intolerance which continues to be a threat to world peace.

The problem which I, and many, many others, have with religion is that its basis is an intellectual conundrum. The riddle of life can't be solved by our intellectual pursuit of religious answers to the question. When one cuts through all the concepts and possibilities which religious leaders make, one is still left without answers. We are asked to have faith in, and trust that there is a God, but we don't have much of an idea who or what this supreme being is. The "mind" part of the trinity is left adrift, and the amorphous "soul" takes over.

Yet, despite this major hurdle which religion is not able to overcome, I, like most people, do find religion an important element of life. Attending church is important to me. I come away most often with a sense of enhanced well-being, heightened by good music, good fellowship and an inspirational message.

On a broader note, it is highly conceivable to me that other intelligent life exists within the universe. We need to find such life or it needs to find us. Our scientists need to find a way to speed much faster than the speed of light for exploration beyond our solar system to be practical. To my knowledge, relatively little resources are being devoted to this effect, which is unfortunate.

Finding intelligent life elsewhere in the universe may help in our quest for an understanding of the meaning of life. But such a discovery will certainly provide further hypotheses which will be helpful.

I often ask myself, and sometimes religious leaders, how they would define success in life from a religious perspective.

The common, simplistic answer is "do good so you will get into heaven." This response evokes the vision of the newly departed at the pearly gates being interviewed by Saint Peter. "You've lived a good life on balance, old man, pass on through." This may be intellectually unsatisfying, but my soul likes it and that's good enough for me.

I grew up attending Sunday school, and as I got older, church services at the Hillside Presbyterian Church. It was a relatively small and simple church with an attached hall and, home for the Reverend George Runner, his wife, and legally blind grown daughter. Reverend Runner was minister at this church for my entire boyhood.

Reverend Runner was an energetic, middle-aged man, outgoing and particularly comfortable in relating to teenagers. He knew us all by names, joked with us constantly and threw in advice in his conversations with us in an unassuming and non-threatening way.

He was very well-known and liked in town and served actively on the Board of Education for many years. As teenagers, we liked him because he treated us as adults. One particularly good example of this was in encouraging us to hang out on Friday and Saturday nights at the hall adjoining the church proper. He'd be certain to provide sodas and snacks, a Victrola and records. He'd stop in once or twice during the evening, joke with us and then leave. No other adults were in attendance. These get-togethers were well attended and many of those present had no affiliation with the church. We'd wander in and out, sometimes going across the street to have a nickel sundae at the local drug store counter. Phil Weinick, the druggist, supplied five-cent sundaes to all those under thirteen years of age. We were mostly all teenagers, but he still charged us only a nickel for one scoop of ice cream with a topping, on Friday and Saturday nights.

This activity was in contrast to the dances at the high school. These were highly supervised; there was always an adult looking at you, it seemed. We had to sign in to the gymnasium, and once you left, you couldn't get back in. Reverend Runner's approach was more to our liking, and I don't believe there was any misbehaving.

My teenage years coincided with the most financially bleak years of the Great Depression. Church revenues dwindled, the mortgage on the building went into default, and the church was unable to pay most of Reverend Runner's salary. He took a job in a defense plant to make ends meet, and announced to the congregation that, since he wasn't being paid, he'd give the same sermon every Sunday until conditions improved.

We teenagers thought this was hilarious. We, over a period of time, memorized his sermon, and restated it to him and each other as a type of ongoing ritual. The sermon took exactly twenty minutes to deliver. Some of us had been named Junior Deacons which provided us with the assignment of taking up the collection immediately after the sermon. We had this timed perfectly so that we could go across the street for a nickel sundae and get back to the church in time to take up the collection. I'm not certain when Reverend Runner resumed orating new sermons, but he remained at the church for many years after World War II ended. The Hillside National Bank never foreclosed on the church property. What would a bank do with a church anyway? Somehow, the finances worked out, and the church is still an integral part of the community.

I had only one non-positive interaction with Reverend Runner. Although I played the piano with a certain amount of proficiency, I had never had the opportunity to play a pipe organ, a more complicated and forbidding musical instrument.

The church organ was usually locked, but one Sunday the organist had left the organ unlocked, having practiced the hymns for that Sunday's service a half hour before church time. I seized the moment and boomed out a rendition of "Don't Get Around Much Anymore."

"Missed the Saturday dance. Heard they crowded the floor, couldn't bear it without you, don't get around much anymore."

As I finished the second verse, Reverend Runner bounded into the choir loft. He said nothing. He didn't need to. I stopped playing and sheepishly stalked away. I wondered what the Reverend would do. After the service, he sought me out, and with a stern straight face, said, "You could have played something more appropriate, like "Rock of Ages" if you were giving an impromptu concert. He broke into a smile and walked away.

My religious training as an impressionable teenager obviously was subliminal under Reverend Runner. But he was an important role model and I have always credited him with what religion is about.

Here's one other anecdote which did not previously affect my lifetime relationship to religion, but does reflect an example of the attitude of the time: When I was in the Navy, I, along with about 200 others, were sent by the Navy from various colleges at which we were being trained to be officers, to the College of the Holy Cross, in Worcester Massachusetts.

Colleges were suffering from the lack of students, and the Navy was helping to fill this void by commissioning with the schools for officer training courses.

Holy Cross was, and is, a fine Jesuit school, which at the time, in 1944, was new to the program. The teachers, among the best I have ever encountered, were primarily Catholic priests, except for the professors who taught gunnery, ballistics, aerial navigation, and the like, who tended to be young naval officers.

As luck would have it (this may have been planned by some far-thinking Pentagon officer) only about a third of the assigned contingent were Roman Catholics.

Immediately upon arriving, our whole group was bombarded with Catholic literature in our mail boxes, were informed that we had to attend mass every morning before breakfast, and say a prayer in unison at the start of every class. This didn't sit well with some of the Protestant and Jewish members of the group, and a few parents found out about it and contacted their congressmen. Within a week, Secretary of the Navy James Forrestal appeared on the Holy Cross campus, reviewed us "troops" in dress parade, had some meetings and left. The next day we received a notice from the college president that mass attendance was no longer required as part of the war effort, and there would be no more required prayers in advance of each class. In addition, no more literature was circulated.

This episode was never reported to the press. In today's media environment, it would be big news. I think that everyone involved learned from the experience. The rigidity of view which caused this episode has long since dissipated.

Taken in its entirety, my involvement with religion has not been an intellectual journey, nor a deeply emotional one. Rather, I am left with some fundamental beliefs and the notion that ascribing to some religious persons has helped me be a better person than I might otherwise have been. I hope some of this aura finds its way into the lives of my children, grandchildren and their families.

CREATIVE WRITING AND EXAMPLES

In a previous chapter, I described books I have written and published and writing contests I have won. I wish I could write more. I continue to come up with ideas. Writing is a time-consuming avocation though, I and would need to give up other activities of interest to turn these ideas into the written word. It's a matter of personal priority.

I'm particularly interested in the short, short story, with a trick ending. Just for fun, I've included two such stories in this book as an example of the style which interests me. I hope the reader will enjoy these stories, entitled "Pride of the Village" and "Vacation".

Additionally, I am interested in various business subjects, including the entrepreneurs' struggles in raising small business investment capital. To demonstrate this interest, I've also included herein a short, basic primer which the entrepreneur can use in the capital raising process. It's very basic, but fills a need. Maybe my grandchildren will learn a bit from it.

Perhaps some time in the future, I'll have enough material for two more books, one a collection of short stories, and the other a compendium of business articles. Time will tell. In the meantime, perhaps the examples included here will serve as examples of an avocation of which I have gained some measure of satisfaction and enjoyment.

PRIDE OF THE VILLAGE

Ovid Banks was dead. Harveyville, New York's eighty-nine-year-old benefactor was suddenly gone, nine years after he returned to his birthplace. The hot, still air in the village funeral parlor suited the occasion, as most of the 600 villagers filed dutifully and quietly past the bier.

Afterwards, out on the sidewalk, they formed little groups and headed down Main Street toward the church where the memorial service was to be held. Past the new library, firehouse and village hall they walked, looking with continuing pride at the imposing structures Ovid had donated to the village. Although the buildings were ostentatious and incongruous grouped with the old and poorly painted houses and stores which dotted the community, few villagers noticed this. They were proud of their village, fiercely proud of their new buildings, the largest and finest in three counties.

Clarence Fuller, the local pharmacist, summed up their feelings as he strolled along with Mayor Bushings.

"No one's weeping, Bush," he said. "For all he did for the village, no one really liked Ovid. Sure, we're proud of what he did, but deep down we still wonder why in hell he ever came back here and spent all that money on us."

"I know, Clarence, but you know the old saying, 'Never look a gift horse in the mouth.'"

"Yep, but he was so ornery. You said yourself that you had a lot of trouble with him."

"True," the mayor agreed. They walked on a few paces before he continued, with a slight chuckle. "I remember when we dedicated the village hall. Morning of the dedication, Ovid called me up. Said as guest of honor he wasn't going to show up unless we tore out the petunias in front of the building. Never liked petunias, he said. Well, I got Jim Fredon down there in a hurry. He pulled out all the petunias and put in some other damn flower. Just got the job done in time. Ovid never said another word about it, and I got stuck paying for the flowers."

"Strange man, crotchety as all get out," Clarence agreed, nodding. "Used to think it was 'cause he was getting old, but I don't rightly know. Right after he came back to the village, he came into the store. Ripped his coat pocket on my stand of picture postcards by the door. He raised all sorts of Cain with my wife behind the counter. Made some remark about who would want a postcard from Harveyville anyway. My wife said she felt like telling him we were all proud of Harveyville even if he wasn't, and if he wasn't, why'd he come back anyway? But she kept her mouth shut."

"Yep, guess there's lots of stories like that people could tell."

"Bush, the trouble with Ovid was he wanted to buy his way into being one of us. We were supposed to bow down to him just because he spent all that money, no matter how he acted. That's why there's no crying today. We're here 'cause of the buildings and 'cause it's the proper thing to do, that's all."

"You're right, Clarence, but it's the end of an era nonetheless. Just look at these buildings. Cost almost $3,000,000. That's more than what everything else in this place is worth put together. Besides the money he gave every year to maintain them. Needed that to keep taxes from going sky high. Since he had no family, expect we'll get enough from his estate to take care of them forever. We should find out about the will later today."

"Wonder why he did it, Bush, he had no real roots in the village. In fact you know he was supposed to have been just about run out of town back when he was eighteen. Nobody was proud of him then either."

"Well, there's lots of rumors 'bout that all right, but no one knows for sure. S'pose after he made all that money and nobody to leave it to he figured he might as well come back here to spend it. Would have all gone to taxes if he'd kept it."

"Yeah, but why pick us? That's what I can't figure."

"Dunno. Pride. Wanting to be part of us. I don't know. Ovid sure was close-mouthed 'bout his reasons. Even though I was Mayor the whole time he was here and had lots of dealings with him, he never confided in me 'bout how he felt 'bout anything. I never pushed him. 'Never look a gift horse in the mouth' always was my motto when it came to Ovid."

The two men reached the church, overflowing with the curious, the idle, and primarily those proud villagers who felt it their duty to be at the service.

One resident of importance was absent. Frank Grant, the local attorney, was standing behind his office desk in the dilapidated building across from the church. He turned away from the desk and stared blankly out the window at the crowded church. On his desk lay a thick legal-size document. It had just been delivered to him, special delivery, registered mail, from a New York City law firm. The document was Ovid's will.

Frank stared for some minutes out the window, through the open church doors at the respectful gathering, down the street at the imposing structures Ovid had built, at the dusty, dilapidated buildings elsewhere along the avenue.

Finally, Frank turned around, picked up the document and again read the paragraph.

"And to the Village of Harveyville which renounced me as a youth, accepted without appreciation my largesse as an old man, and rejected me as an individual and community member always, I bequeath the annual debt of maintenance on the property previously provided by me, which debt shall stand as a constant reminder of the treatment accorded me by the people of Harveyville."

"My God," sighed Frank. "Maintenance will triple our taxes. The old man has bankrupted us." He turned again to face the window as the church bell began to peal.

VACATION

On the final day of their joint vacation, the two young couples played five sets of tennis, swam twenty lengths of the pool against a stopwatch, and after dinner, completed three rubbers of bridge. Susan Bruhl and Douglas Arends defeated their respective spouses, Harry and Barbara, at all five tennis sets and in all three rubbers of bridge, as well as in the swimming heats. They were now well into the fourth rubber of bridge and Susan and Douglas were again, not surprisingly, in the lead. It had been that way all week.

The four had been friends since childhood, and after each had married three years earlier, in weddings that were conveniently spaced just one month apart, their friendship had grown deeper. Inspired by the freedom each couple experienced as newlyweds, and by their complete compatibility, they spent much of their leisure time together. They learned to ride horses, play badminton and tennis, ride surfboards, ski. Together they took golf lessons, bridge lessons, and had even studied French in contemplation of a vaguely planned European holiday.

Both women had promising careers in marketing. Their husbands were climbing the corporate ladder in separate companies. Each couple's combined incomes totaled approximately the same per year, and all such information they exchanged cheerfully, confiding to each other the progress of their respective savings accumulations. They even planned to have their children at the same time, each intending to wait until their savings totaled fifty thousand dollars. They still had eighteen months to reach that goal.

"Wouldn't it be a kick to have our first child on the same day as you!" Barbara exclaimed one evening, as they compared their savings account balances. "The children could be as close as we are." The three others nodded and smiled their agreement. They even planned to name their first born after one or the other of their friends, depending upon the sex.

At the hotel, the two couples had, in their week's stay, become the subject of conversation among the other guests.

"Have you noticed those two young couples who are always together?" a bejeweled and heavily-rouged old lady remarked to the young mother who had taken the wicker rocker on the porch next to hers. The latter had stationed herself there in order to watch her five-year-old examine the garden flowers. "Always doing something," the old lady continued. "Tennis, swimming, boating, dancing. I don't know how they keep it up."

"It is a puzzlement," the young woman agreed, tired from simply watching her little boy play.

As she threaded her way to her table in the dining room, a middle-aged matron greeted an elderly couple seated at one of the tables with, "Good morning. I wonder what our two young couples will do today?"

An older widower, intent upon impressing the assorted unattached females with his wit, likened the activities of the two pairs to Olympic performers. "I think they're trying to break the world decathlon record," he remarked one evening, with a wink, sending his audience into fits of laughter, including several of his contemporaries who had no notion what decathlon meant.

The competition between the two couples had begun quite innocently. It was Harry who had started it all two years earlier when they decided to take bridge lessons together.

"Let's keep track of each couple's scores, how 'bout it?" he suggested.

"Um…we could do that, but shouldn't we split up?" Susan wondered out loud. "That would make it more fun."

So it was settled. The idea spread to include every competitive activity they engaged in together. At first the scores, which Susan kept cumulatively in a big notebook, were quite even. Gradually, however, she and Douglas pulled away into commanding, then unsurmountable leads. During this last week of vacation, Barbara and Harry had failed miserably to win at anything.

"That's okay, Harry," Barbara sympathized, patting him on the back. "Unlucky at cards, lucky at love."

"Maybe," Harry answered, "but I'm afraid we've been unlucky at more than just cards."

Susan and Douglas ignored the remark and continued to tease their opponents unmercifully as the slaughter continued.

Finally, the four of them were alone in the game room. Most of the other guests had retired for the night, but they played on.

"Last rubber," Susan noted, shuffling the cards. "And we're vulnerable." She dealt the cards deftly and quickly sorted them. "Two hearts," she bid.

Harry passed, but Douglas bid four hearts, and the others passed.

"Well, this is it," Susan announced, confidently. Then she laughed.

"I underbid, partner," Douglas said smugly, laying his hand down on the table. He grinned at Barbara who sat beside him. "How many rubbers in a row is that for this week? Twenty-one?"

"Almost as many as tennis sets," Susan declared, her eyes sparkling. "Let's see now," she continued, pulling a sheet of paper from her handbag and consulting it thoughtfully. "We've won nineteen rubbers of bridge, not counting this one, which is obviously a lay down. In tennis, it's twenty-four sets in a row. In badminton, Doug and I have taken twelve straight games. In swimming…"

"Oh, go to hell," Harry muttered. He stood, threw his cards on the table, and walked with measured steps out of the room. Susan's anxious eyes followed her husband as he disappeared into the lobby. The three who remained fell into an uncomfortable, strained silence.

"Well, I guess the tournament's over," Susan finally managed, forcing a smile. "Good night, folks. See you at breakfast." She got up and followed her husband to her room.

At his christening, nine months later, Harry Bruhl, Jr. did not even cry.

DOES YOUR ANGEL INVESTOR WEAR A HALO?

So you have found a potential angel investor to provide financing to help the development of your business. Great! But how certain are you that the relationship is likely to be a compatible and mutually gratifying one? Sure, the financial terms seem appealing, and the use of the proceeds is well defined and timely. But are your respective expectations similar? Is the investor's exit time requirement realistic from your perspective? Are your personalities compatible? Can, and will, the investor provide strategic advice and encouragement as well as financial support? In other words, will your angel investor wear a halo?

Here are some thoughts to aid you in navigating through the process of selecting an angel investor. Of course, you will need an attorney to prepare an agreement outlining the financial terms of the investment. But there are other factors to consider which are not readily included in a written agreement.

1. <u>Fully Understanding the Investor's Goals and Expectations</u>

    Beware of the investor, individually or through a fund under his or her control, who expects a twenty-five percent annual compounded rate of return with a five year exit window. That theoretical requirement may be unrealistic. Angels often need to be more patient. Talk this out in advance. While you need to respect the investor's exit goals (and you may even want to exit on the same time frame as the investor), your primary focus needs to be growing the business. A required exit can be inhibiting to your own strategies. Exiting is an ongoing dynamic during the relationship worthy of continuing communication. Good angels wear their halos with a patient, yet watchful eye.

2. <u>Agreeing on Risk Tolerance Strategy</u>

    Often the potential for faster growth requires higher risk. Discuss your strategic plan with the investor (it's a good idea to write out a plan that strategizes how you intend to grow). You and your investor need to have an initial agreement on strategy, and ongoing dialogue as circumstances evolve.

3. <u>The Investor's Financial Resources</u>

    You need to have some idea how important financially, as well as emotionally, the proposed investment is to your angel. Is this just one of many investments? Are any other investments compatible or conflicting with your own business? Can, and will, the investor consider additional investments in your company? Is the angel the sole provider of the investment?

4. <u>Succession</u>

    Circumstances change. Discuss what will happen if one of you becomes incapacitated or dies. Some of these potentialities can be covered in a stockholders agreement which your attorney can prepare. But each of you should consider the possibilities and talk them over. A written agreement can establish ground rules, but you will want to review various scenarios.

5. <u>Helping You Beyond the Money</u>

    Angels come from different backgrounds with diverse experiences, contacts, and varying desires to help you beyond a financial commitment. Industry and other business contacts may be shared. Introducing your angel to potential customers, bank loan officers, potential merger candidates and possible hires could prove beneficial to you.

6. <u>Operating Procedures</u>

    You and your angel investor will want to define how and when you will communicate. How involved does the investor want or need to be in day-to-day operations? What decisions need to be made jointly? What financial reports will be required? Discuss these matters in advance of finalizing the arrangement. Keeping track of cash flow is probably the most important recurring reporting requirement.

7. <u>Choosing Advisors</u>

    Your business relies on outside advisors on various matters. Agreement should be reached on employing attorneys, accountants, bankers, insurance providers and any other professional support you may require. Building a team is important.

8. <u>The Overall Relationship</u>

    Angels may or may not be of the "guardian" type. Relationships differ. You and your angel need to be comfortable with each other, have an understanding and respect for each other's goals and motivations. The relationship between you and an angel who is a relative compared to one that is developed through internet crowd sourcing is very different. And in between these two examples are vast distinctions which require both you and your angel to develop your own personalized arrangement. The more you communicate both in advance of finalizing the arrangement, and in continuing discussions throughout the investment period the more "heavenly" the relationship will be.

THOUGHTS ABOUT THE PAST

There have been eight major decisions which have shaped my life. None were solely of my own choosing, but each required thought and definitive action on my part. Here is a summary of each of these choices and how each has affected my life.

<u>College Education</u>

There never was any question of going to college as I grew up. Both my parents were college graduates who believed strongly in education, so that the question of college was where to go and not should I go.

In 1943, admission to college was relatively easy. World War II was raging and college enrollment was greatly reduced due to armed service requirements for all males over eighteen years of age. Only those pre medical, pre ministerial and physically challenged were deferred from military service, so college enrollments suffered.

I had no idea where I should go to college or what I should study. I knew I preferred liberal arts subjects rather than math and science, and was encouraged, particularly by my mother, to concentrate on English.

I visited three colleges as a high school senior – Princeton, Dartmouth and Colgate. Princeton was the most prestigious nearby university, Dartmouth was recommended by friends and Colgate was the alma mater of Wilbur Cox, my high school principal. We had no counselors then to advise us, but Mr. Cox took an interest in me and suggested I consider Colgate.

I liked all three schools I visited. Princeton vaguely seemed too close to home and Dartmouth appeared to be somewhat remote at a time when transportation, due to gas rationing, was substantially curtailed.

So, at Wilbur Cox's urging, I agreed to go to Colgate, although I had been accepted at Princeton and Dartmouth as well. I don't recall my parents exerting any influence one way or another. They let me make my own decision at seventeen years old.

In retrospect, I don't think the decision was particularly important. All were good schools and I would have received good liberal arts educations at each. But this was really my first independent decision of importance in my life, and I thought it was a momentous one at the time.

Armed Service

As I approached eighteen years of age, I had to make a decision on whether to be drafted into the Army, or enlist in either the Navy or Marine Corps.

In making this decision, my parents were of no help at all. My mother's advice was to delay entering the armed services as long as possible, hoping the war would soon be over and the service requirement ended.

As a senior in high school, I had taken a test to become eligible for a college based officer training program sponsored by the Army and Navy which at the time was considered a very elite program. My mother vehemently objected to my entering this program which would have begun immediately upon my high school graduation, soon after my seventeenth birthday. Her view was to delay my going into the service as long as possible, and enlisting in this program would have put me in service a year earlier even though it would have been at a college, and not anywhere on the war front.

Only a few of us high school seniors passed the test and I was the only one to pass up the opportunity. So I headed off to Colgate as a civilian, rather than as an officer trainee at the college of the government's choice.

But I had to make a decision as I approached eighteen. I didn't want to go into the Army and the government training program wasn't available to me since I had turned it down. So, on my own, with no outside advice, including my parents, I enlisted in the U.S. Naval Reserve just before my eighteenth birthday, and as I completed my freshman year at Colgate.

I was never enamored by joining the armed services. Many considered it an adventure. I considered it something I was required to do. I thought the discipline was mind debilitating and limited one's potential.

My Navy career, as I have described it elsewhere in this memoir, turned out to be just fine. The federal government paid for much of my education, saving my parents a considerable amount. I learned much in areas I would never have studied as a civilian (nautical navigation and advance gunnery are two examples), and in how to motivate large groups of diverse people into being one cohesive force.

I made a good decision on joining the Navy. But good luck had much to do with this short career. I think I had developed more maturity than many of my peers, I worked hard to meet the expectations of my superiors, and I was blessed by the sudden end of World War II enabled by the development and use of the atomic bomb.

If it were not for the invention of the bomb, I would have been a junior naval officer on a small boat hopping from island to island in the Pacific on a slow path to defeating Japan under constant threat of air and sea gunfire.

Marriage

Certainly the most important decision of my life, and my very best one, was marrying June. Nothing comes close to the joy she has added to my life. I've dedicated an entire chapter to our marriage, and could have written a complete book on our life together, and perhaps I will do so in the future.

Where to Live

June and I always lived in one-family houses in suburban areas as we grew up and married. We had a taste of apartment living during the first year of our marriage, and quickly decided that buying a home in a suburban environment was a top priority.

We had saved about $5,000 and, after looking in various areas, settled on Madison, New Jersey, a commuters' town with train service directly into New York City.

Madison, N.J. Train Station

Construction was booming and Madison was expanding rapidly, led by "starter" homes attractive to the great number of newly married war veterans. The federal government was encouraging home buying through mortgage guarantees from the Federal Housing Administration.

We bought a new two bedroom, five room home with an expandable second floor for $13,000, financing it with a $10,000 four percent Federal Housing Administration GI mortgage. We were scared of the financial responsibility, but my father kept assuring us that it was a sound move. After all, he told us, you're putting thirty percent of the purchase price down and your mortgage is less than your combined annual income. He, of course, was right. Our confidence grew and within five years we had purchased a building lot in the "hill" region of Madison for $5,000, committed to build a much larger home for $23,500 and sell our "starter" home at a thirty percent profit. Subsequently, we added a family room, fifth bedroom and another bath to this home which we still live in today. It's worth fifty times what we paid for it, so financially it was a good decision. Even more important, though, we have found Madison to be a wonderful place to live, raise children, and make friends. There's some luck involved in making real estate decisions, but location is the most important attribute.

In addition to our Madison home, we have made financially and emotionally good decisions in acquiring seashore and Florida vacation homes. We find living on the water very relaxing and values continue to rise as the population expands. Once the coastlines have been fully developed, there is no more property on which to build. Demand grows, but the inventory of available waterfront property remains the same. Perhaps global warming will eventually negatively affect such property, but in the meantime, we, and our families are enjoying the waterfronts.

Community Service

Participating in volunteer, community, nonprofit activity has always been an important part of my life, important enough that I have devoted an entire chapter to it in this book. Deciding on which organizations in which to participate is an ongoing challenge, dependent upon where one's interest lies, where the need is great, where one's skills can make a positive difference, and where one can work well with others instilling goals and implementing them. Altogether, volunteering can be a most satisfying and fruitful lifetime activity.

Four Children

June and I made our decisions on having children one at a time. There was never a pre-marriage discussion on the subject. The decisions were based on our physical and financial capacities at the time. This book contains a chapter on growing our family. We had our children at a time when four was a typical number. We didn't think about how this would double the population in one generation if each set of newlyweds made the same decision.

Career

Other than marriage and children, choosing a career is perhaps the most important decision of one's life. I use the word "perhaps" in this regard since it can be argued that one's talents and shortcomings will affect whichever career path one chooses, so success and failure would be similar no matter what profession one engages in. This is a big subject, and one to which an entire chapter is dedicated.

Retirement Activities

Each of us is different. Our physical and mental health varies, as do our individual temperaments and motivations.

But there are a few basic retirement criteria which apply to each of us "retired" persons.

The first rule should be to discard the word "retired". While most of us have concluded a career and are receiving a pension and social security, most of us continue to be very active. Whether this activity is in some money making pursuit, community services, or absorbing hobby is up to the individual.

An increasing number of those completing careers have a twenty-five-year period of potentially fruitful activity before them.

To just drift through this period without a sense of purpose seems to me to be a waste of one's potential.

So my second rule is to plan one's retirement to meet a set of objectives including, perhaps a need or desire for additional income, satisfaction from applying an entrepreneurial spirit to building a business, mentoring and consulting to those who could gain from your experiences, story and essay writing, and in volunteer charity work that can provide you with the satisfaction of making a positive difference in the lives of others.

In my case, I have combined a number of activities to fit my own desires. I have, with others, made venture capital investments which have been financially successful and which have utilized my financial training and experiences. I have continued with charitable endeavors, although to a lesser extent than when I was active in my career. I have written several unpublished short stories and have an outline for a book on the accounting profession. I also have outlined the plot for a novel, but don't have any confidence that I have much talent in that area of writing. I'm still serving on a few corporate boards of directors and will continue to do so until the companies tell me I'm no longer contributing positively.

I've always enjoyed gardening. A neat and vibrant garden that I have created gives me great satisfaction. And, I have been collecting postage stamps throughout my life which I hope someone will become interested enough in organizing them into albums.

Those various efforts meet my individual needs, keep my mind busy, and blend into a set of "retirement" activities which I find challenging, productive and satisfying.

I certainly have been blessed with good fortune throughout life. Born into a middle class environment, in a great country, encouraged and provided with opportunities by caring parents, marrying happily – these attributes, aided by some lucky occurrences, have shaped a life that has been truly blessed in a world that has deprived many of the opportunities I have enjoyed, creating sadness and despair in their lives. I offer my thanks to all those who have shared their own lives with me. My hope is that those less fortunate will somehow find the way to a life of opportunity as I have.

THOUGHTS ABOUT THE FUTURE

We are living in an exciting era. New nations and economics are developing, the internet has created new, and in many cases, eliminated age-old occupations. Immigration is increasing. Intermarriage among races and religions is spreading, medical research is promising to end heretofore untreatable diseases, artificial intelligence is becoming more usable in daily life, and exploration outside our solar system is underway.

Given all these changes, and recognizing the changes they inevitably bring, can cause discomfort and concern as well as awe. It is fitting, in a memoir, to suggest what might lie ahead that will impact the lives of one's grandchildren and great grandchildren. It's always fun to act as a prophet, but it will also be interesting for grandchildren and potential great grandchildren to compare these predictions with actuality seventy-five to one hundred years from now.

So here are my thoughts on some major developments which may occur within the next century:

1. Many life-threatening diseases will be eliminated or substantially controlled, including diabetes, many forms of cancer, most dementia and others.
2. Some form of human life as we now know it will be discovered on a planet in another solar system within our galaxy. We will learn little from this discovery inasmuch as the civilizations will be less advanced than ours.
3. A universal language, both written and oral, will be developed and begin to be used worldwide.
4. There will be a proliferation of nuclear bomb capability among nations, which somehow will promote more peaceful relationships.
5. The United States of America will continue to dominate the world economically, and will out of necessity devote much of its resources to aiding other nations – a sort of international socialism.
6. Fossil fuels will no longer be a source of energy, thus substantially reducing the impact of global warming.
7. Most automobiles will have driverless functions.

8. The major religions of the world will create a role much like the Pope. This group will meet annually to promote peace and acceptance of each other's faith. Differences among religions will fade to a major extent, although more individual sects will develop to meet the perceived needs of localized cultures.

9. In American politics, the two-party system will continue to dominate. However, both parties will edge toward more progressive policies, fueled by the continuing inability of the democratic process to solve the persistent and increasing gap in incomes.

10. The United States of America will elect its first non-white female as president.

11. Individuals with Latino backgrounds will become a majority, but it will be difficult to categorize people due to large increases in intermarriage among races and ethnic backgrounds.

12. A vast majority of Americans will finally agree that global warming exists and will back measures to cope with this threat.

13. Barack Obama will be named as one of our great presidents based upon his views and actions concerning healthcare and immigration.
14. The national deficit will remain relatively static. Increasing benefit expenditures, increasing social security and healthcare will largely be offset by increased productivity.
15. Many more will work from home. Office rentals will tumble.
16. Retirement age will generally increase to age seventy-five, and many retired workers will continue working to age eighty-five.
17. More than half those receiving long term, consistent healthcare will live to age ninety-five or older.
18. June and I will have forty great grandchildren who will live to an average age in excess of one hundred years.
19. Strict laws banning assault weapons and requiring background checks for any gun purchases will be passed by Congress.
20. Two years college tuition will become an entitlement to those who pass service qualifications. Private college tuitions will soar, pricing all but the financially elite out of the market.

21. Labor unions will enjoy a resurgence, buoyed by a robust economy and the need to organize new kinds of jobs.
22. The United States and China will become allies, based upon their strengths and mutual goals and concerns. Most of the Far East will continue to grow.
23. The world's population will at least double, causing persistent, localized food shortages.
24. Universal health care will become a reality in the USA.
25. Social media will take on new forms and become the most important means of communicating.
26. Artificial intelligence will take over stock market analysis. The resulting data will be more accurate than could be gleaned from human study.

Okay, great grandchildren, how good a prophet was your great grandfather? All forty of you should participate in this exercise. Each prognostication is worth four points. Your great grandfather was a genius if he scored eighty.

One last thing, how many of you can name all of your cousins and their birthdays? If there are forty of you, you need to get thirty of the names and birthdates right if you want to be considered a close family relative.